D1083103

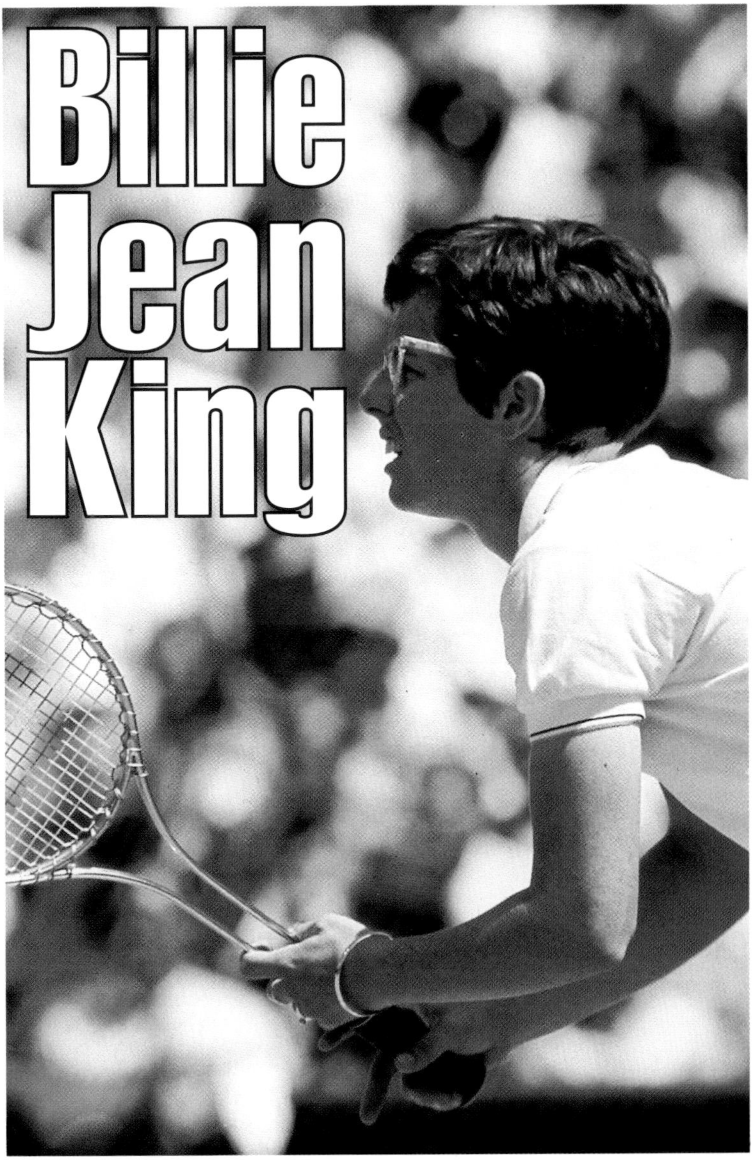
Billie
Jean
King

Billie Jean King

TENNIS TRAILBLAZER

by Joanne Lannin

Lerner Publications Company • Minneapolis

To Don Murray

Copyright © 1999 Joanne Lannin

Website address: www.lernerbooks.com

Library of Congress Cataloging-in-Publication Data

Lannin, Joanne.
   Billie Jean King : tennis trailblazer / by Joanne Lannin.
     p.   cm.
   Includes bibliographical references (p.   ) and index.
   Summary: A biography of one of the first women to play tennis professionally.
   ISBN 0-8225-4959-X (alk. paper)
   1. King, Billie Jean—Juvenile literature. 2. Tennis players—United States—Biography—Juvenile literature. [1. King, Billie Jean. 2. Tennis players. 3. Women—Biography.] I. Title.
GV994.K56 L35 1999
796.342'092—dc21
  [B]   98–37488

Manufactured in the United States of America
1 2 3 4 5 6 – JR – 04 03 02 01 00 99

CONTENTS

Bill Moffitt poses with his active little daughter, Billie Jean.

BILLIE JEAN FINDS TENNIS

BILLIE JEAN MOFFITT LEANED OUT THE PASSEN-
ger window of her mother's convertible and watched a
row of eucalyptus trees go by. Ahead, on the right, she
saw two gray cement tennis courts and a man beside
them with a clipboard in his hands. Billie Jean cradled
her new wooden tennis racket in her lap and clasped
its lavender handle tightly as the car slowed to a stop
beside the courts. It was a clear, sunny day in September 1954 and Billie Jean, 10 years old, was about to
take her first tennis lesson.

The Long Beach, California, Recreation Department's
municipal courts were full of kids wanting to learn to
play tennis. Billie Jean was as eager as any of them.
She had mowed lawns and run errands all summer to
earn the $8 for her racket, one that would cost more

Betty and Bill Moffitt

than $50 in the 1990s. Billie Jean was hoping to learn the game of tennis as a substitute for softball and football, two sports her parents had persuaded her to give up. Both Billie Jean and her younger brother, Randy, had acquired a competitive fire and a love of athletics from their father, Bill Moffitt, a firefighter and engineer at the local fire station. Bill, a tall, square-jawed man with blue eyes and wavy brown hair, had been an athlete in high school. He continued to play basketball with men his age while Billie Jean and Randy were growing up. He took the games seriously, arguing calls as vehemently as an NBA coach would. While her mother cringed in the stands, Billie Jean would nod and point proudly in her father's direction when someone asked if that was her dad out there.

Billie Jean was born on November 22, 1943. Her mother, Betty, had thought she would name a baby girl Michelle Louise. But Bill Moffitt was called off to serve in World War II just before the baby was born. Betty decided she had better name this one after him. Billie Jean remained an only child until her brother Randy came along in 1948. After his birth, Billie Jean's nickname soon became "Sis." When Billie Jean was

Billie Jean Moffitt, just five years old, holds her baby brother, Randy, in this family photograph.

four, she and her dad began spending hours in the
backyard of their neat house on West 36th Street,
throwing a rubber baseball back and forth.

Bill carved Billie Jean her own baseball bat out of a
piece of wood. After supper, Bill would pull his stop-
watch out of a drawer and time the neighborhood kids
in the 60-yard dash—from a playhouse up the street to
the tree in front of the
Moffitt house. From early
on, sports were a way for
Billie Jean to break out of
the shyness she sometimes
felt in school. While she liked school, she hated having to give reports in front of the class. Maybe it was
the fact that she was so much bigger than all the other
girls and most of the boys in her class. Her self-con-
sciousness made it easy to trip over words and forget
what she was trying to say.

**I'M GOING TO DO SOMETHING
WONDERFUL.**

Despite her lack of confidence in front of the class,
Billie Jean did feel from an early age that there was
something special about her. One day when she was
five, she told her mother so. Billie Jean burst into the
kitchen to proclaim, "I'm going to do something wonderful."

For a while, Billie Jean was interested in playing
piano. Not long after she started school, she begged
her parents to buy a piano so she could take lessons
like some of the other kids in her class. Billie Jean's
mother had played violin as a child and was glad to

hear that her daughter was interested in music. So the Moffitts saved up for a piano that Billie Jean faithfully played every day after supper.

Sports were still Billie Jean's number one interest, though. By the age of 10, Billie Jean could throw a softball farther and faster from shortstop to first base than most 15-year-old girls. She had helped her softball team win the all-city championship that summer by making a diving catch and then leaping up to throw to third base for a game-ending double play.

Football was the most popular game in her neighborhood and it was a game Billie Jean excelled in. Her muscular legs made her a fast, strong, running back and the best place-kicker in neighborhood games. One day, she amazed the adults watching on the sidelines by kicking a long field goal to win a game in the last seconds of play.

Both Billie Jean and her younger brother had athletic talent. While Randy began working toward a professional pitching career from an early age, Billie Jean found herself wondering where her talent would take her. Billie Jean's parents were afraid she would get hurt playing football with boys who would soon be bigger and stronger than she was. Softball, with all that sliding and diving for balls, also seemed unladylike to Billie Jean's mother. Basketball didn't seem to be an option either. Billie Jean was asked to quit her elementary school team because she was so big and strong that the other players couldn't stop her from scoring and couldn't get any rebounds away from her.

As Billie Jean and her mother washed and dried the supper dishes together one night, Mrs. Moffitt suggested to her daughter that she find a sport, like golf or swimming, that she could play long into adulthood. But golf seemed too slow and Billie Jean was too afraid of water to be a good swimmer. Then her father suggested tennis. "You run a lot and you hit a ball," he explained. Billie Jean knew nothing about the game, but this sounded good to her. She decided to give it a try.

Billie Jean's coach for that first tennis lesson was Clyde Walker, a man in his 60s who had been a teaching professional at country clubs most of his life. He had given that up recently to teach on the city's public courts. He was tired of teaching the children of wealthy country-club patrons, some of whom seemed to be there only to pass the time while their parents played golf or ate lunch at the club.

Walker hoped to find on the municipal courts some youngsters who were really eager to learn the game. When Billie Jean told him she was only 10, Walker smiled and told her it was great that she wanted to learn. By the end of that first lesson, Billie Jean was smiling, too. She'd learned how to grip the racket properly and how good it felt to hit the ball squarely on the sweet spot in the middle of the strings. When the hour was up and her mother came to drive her home, she asked Billie Jean how the lesson had gone.

"Great, just great," Billie Jean told her. "I want to play tennis forever. I want to be the number one tennis player in the world."

At first, Billie Jean played tennis the way she approached any sport—with unbridled excitement. Walker had to break her of the habit of rushing to the net for every shot. She was so excited and so impatient that she tried to hit every ball before it hit the ground. Slowly, he taught her how to stay back at the baseline and use her ground strokes.

> I WANT TO PLAY TENNIS FOREVER. I WANT TO BE THE NUMBER ONE TENNIS PLAYER IN THE WORLD.

A few months after her lessons began, Billie Jean and her fellow students competed in a novice tournament that Walker held to introduce them to competition. Billie Jean hadn't yet learned how to serve the ball from over her head. She lost the first match to another beginner 6–0, 6–0. (See scoring, page 127.) By June of 1955, just nine months after her lessons had begun, Walker suggested to Billie Jean that it was time for her to enter her first real tournament, the Southern California Junior Championships. For this first junior tournament, 11-year-old Billie Jean played in the 13-and-under division. She beat her first opponent, who was ranked 17th in Southern California's junior division, in straight sets. But in her second match, she lost two sets to one. The third set was a heartbreaker that Billie Jean lost 9–7. Billie Jean had blisters on her feet.

She realized on the way home that tennis was going to be more work than she'd thought.

She was determined to get better, fast. She began following Walker around the city—taking lessons from him on Tuesdays at the courts near her house and on other days in different parts of the city. Walker spent extra time with Billie Jean, even on the weekends when she played tennis from nine in the morning until dark. Walker told her he was delighted that he'd finally found someone as enthusiastic and dedicated to tennis as he was.

When she wasn't playing tennis, Billie Jean read everything she could about the sport and the stars who played it. She watched matches on television whenever she could. While watching, she would practice her ground strokes in the living room—now and then knocking over the living room lamp. Outside, Billie Jean hit the tennis ball so often and so hard against the wooden fence in the backyard that her father finally tore it down and replaced it with a wall made out of cement blocks.

Billie Jean was spending so much time on tennis that her piano lessons were suffering. She had convinced her parents to buy the piano but now she was telling her mother she had to quit. Mrs. Moffitt insisted that Billie Jean stick with piano lessons until she could read music and play some songs by heart. She wanted to teach Billie Jean to finish what she started. Still, Mrs. Moffitt could see for herself, in

Billie Jean was active in many clubs and organizations as a teenager. She is the second from the left in the back row in this picture of her high school sorority.

those hours she spent at the park watching her daughter play tennis, that tennis was Billie Jean's passion. By the time Billie Jean was in her early teens and entering tournaments regularly, her parents agreed to let her give up piano lessons and concentrate on tennis.

The hard work began to pay off. By 1958, Billie Jean was the number two girl in the 15-and-under Southern California division. As usual, her dreams were much bigger. "I never thought of myself as a junior," she wrote in her first autobiography in 1974. "I always thought of myself as part of the bigger world of top women's tennis."

Betty Moffitt made many of Billie Jean's tennis outfits, including the one Billie Jean is wearing in this photograph.

COMING OF AGE

THE LATE 1950s WERE A GOOD TIME TO BE COM-ing of age in women's tennis. Some of the great women of the game, such as Althea Gibson and Maureen Connolly, were retiring. There was space at the top for girls like Billie Jean. That doesn't mean Billie Jean's road to stardom was smoothly paved. She was different from the young women the tennis circuit was accustomed to. Tennis in the 1950s was a prim and proper game with a strict dress code of white polo shirts and shorts for men and white pleated dresses for ladies. Audiences clapped politely at winning points. Competitors smiled gracefully, win or lose. Billie Jean had been shy in front of a class as a child, but during tennis matches she lost her inhibitions and found her voice. She whooped and shouted after winning points, often making more noise talking to herself than the people in the stands made watching her.

Billie Jean came from a different background than most of the players facing her across the net. Most of them had parents who belonged to the local country club. Many had horses of their own and their own tennis courts. Though Billie Jean was fiercely proud of her family, she couldn't help but feel her background was inferior to that of many of the other tennis players. Billie Jean's mother, Betty, stayed at home while her husband often worked the night shift at the fire station. He was an engineer who passed up promotions so he could continue to do the work he loved. Betty Moffitt saved up money for some luxuries, like their piano and their 1947 Chevy convertible, by sewing the kids' clothes, hooking rugs and selling Avon products and Tupperware. Still, the Moffitt household was a modest one, where springs occasionally popped through the couch cushions and the rugs were worn threadbare.

Once Billie Jean began entering tournaments outside the Long Beach area in 1958, her father got a second job in a plastics factory. They needed the money to fill the car's gas tank every weekend and to help pay for tournament entry fees. Billie Jean didn't dress the way other girls did. In fact, she was barred from a junior team photo by a local U. S. Lawn Tennis Association (USLTA) official, Perry Jones, because of the way she dressed. Instead of a white tennis dress, Billie Jean wore shorts that her mother had sewn for her. Billie Jean wore out her white tennis shoes so quickly that her mother wrapped the toes of the shoes in adhesive tape so they would last a little longer.

Perry Jones was president of the Southern California Tennis Association and one of the most powerful men in the U. S. Lawn Tennis Association. He was a big, slightly overweight man who always wore suspenders and usually had on dark sunglasses and a wide-brimmed straw hat. The junior players knew that if they didn't toe the line for Jones, they could forget about getting any breaks when it came to tennis. One of the biggest disappointments of Billie Jean's young tennis life came in 1958 when, at the age of 14, she didn't have the money to compete in the USLTA's women's summer circuit on the East Coast. Other girls her age were competing over the summer, as a way to gain valuable experience. Their families paid their travel expenses and entry fees, considering it a different kind of summer camp.

It took all the money her family could afford to send Billie Jean and her mother to just one tournament—the U. S. Junior Nationals in Middletown, Ohio—early that summer. Jones, who oversaw how sponsor money was distributed to the juniors, could have helped Billie Jean with her expenses. He wasn't a mean man, but he was a stickler for tradition and the rules. He insisted that Billie Jean had to have a chaperone to go to Ohio. Even though Billie Jean had beaten the number one junior tennis player in Southern California a few weeks before, Jones said that the tennis association would only pay for Billie Jean's expenses and not her mother's.

A group of tennis patrons came through with some money, but not enough to allow Billie Jean's mother to fly along with her. So Billie Jean and her mother took a train cross-country to Ohio. Billie Jean lost in the quarterfinals of the Junior Nationals. While the other young women, from families whose parents could afford to pay their way, proceeded to Philadelphia to play on the women's circuit, Billie Jean and her mother boarded their train for home with only three dollars left in their pockets.

Billie Jean ached to play on the women's circuit. She knew she was better than some of the girls who were making the trip, and she longed to prove it. The incident spurred Billie Jean to improve her game so that she would be the number one junior player in Southern California and assure herself the sponsors she needed to pay for tournament trips.

In school she often daydreamed about playing at international tournaments. When she was 14, she turned one of her daydreams into a school essay, describing in detail the flight across the ocean and the early morning fog that enveloped the court at Wimbledon in Great Britain.

School and society didn't offer Billie Jean much support for her dreams. Male athletes were treated to steak dinners before their games. But Billie Jean had

difficulty convincing her school's principal to allow
her to miss a day of school to go to an out-of-town
tennis match. While her little brother's exploits as a
budding baseball star were winning him praise from
the community, Billie Jean's tennis trophies were
largely ignored outside of her family.

That didn't stop Billie Jean from dreaming and
scheming. She confided in Reverend Bob Richards, the
1952 and 1956 Olympic
pole-vaulting champion.
Richards was the minister
of the church the Moffitts
attended. Billie Jean had

> I'M GOING TO BE THE BEST TENNIS
> PLAYER IN THE WORLD.

also daydreamed about becoming a missionary when
she grew up. She enjoyed Richards's sermons because
he got so emotional and seemed to be talking directly
to her. During the week, she liked to watch him practice pole vaulting in a dirt pit he'd made beside the
church. One day as she stood outside the church
watching him practice, Richards asked her what she
was going to do with her life. She forgot about her re-
ligious aspirations and replied without any hesitation,
"I know exactly what I'm going to do, Reverend. I'm
going to be the best tennis player in the world."

Billie Jean still took lessons from Clyde Walker after
school. A high school sophomore in the fall of 1958,
Billie Jean enjoyed going to high school football games
with kids in her class. But otherwise, her life was too
busy with tennis for activities such as sleepovers or

Bob Richards twice won Olympic gold medals in pole vaulting before becoming an ordained minister.

hanging out at the local drugstore. She walked to school every day with a neighbor, Jerry Cromwell, another student of Walker's who was like a second brother to her. She would tell him her dreams of being a champion tennis player. Cromwell would reply, "Oh Billie Jean, you're just a dumb girl." Billie Jean would argue even as they made their way from their lockers to their first class. "You wait and see," she would say. "I bet I'll change things more than you will."

In the fall of 1959, a Wilson sporting goods salesman arranged for Billie Jean to take lessons with Alice Marble, one of the pioneers of American women's tennis in the 1930s. Marble often tutored up-and-coming young tennis players. Though it meant leaving her first coach, Clyde Walker, Billie Jean and Walker agreed that it was too good an opportunity to pass up. Marble lived in Tarzana, about 40 miles from Long Beach. Billie Jean's mother would drop her off each Saturday and she would stay at Marble's house until Sunday. Alice Marble was the grande dame of women's tennis. She had won at Wimbledon in 1939, was a four-time winner of the U. S. national title, and revolutionized tennis with her aggressive, hard-serving style. In 1950, she also helped break the racial barriers in women's tennis by writing an editorial that accused the USLTA board of governors of racism for failing to allow Althea Gibson, a black woman, to compete at the U. S. Open in Forest Hills, New York. The editorial shocked and then shamed the tennis officials, causing them to reverse their decision and allow Gibson to play.

When Billie Jean met Marble in 1959, Marble was only in her late 40s, but she was suffering from a lung disease. Thin and frail, she had to take oxygen every night. Still, she could spot minor flaws in anyone's tennis game, even from the sidelines. With Marble's help, Billie Jean refined her shot-making and fixed some technical flaws in her serving and volleying techniques. After a day on the court, as they ate dinner or sat and talked, Billie Jean learned what it was like to be a champion. She was enthralled by stories of tennis greats, such as Helen Wills Moody and Bobby Riggs, who Marble had either watched or played. Billie Jean could feel her stomach tighten as Marble described

As an up-and-coming star in 1931, Alice Marble revolutionized women's tennis with her hard-charging style.

playing a pressure-packed match on the Centre Court grass of Wimbledon or at Forest Hills.

Billie Jean also gained a sense of the pride and competitiveness that comes with being a champion. That pride led to a falling out with Marble over two incidents. The first incident took place just a few weeks into the lessons when Billie Jean confessed that her goal was to be the greatest tennis player ever. Marble thought it was arrogant of a student to want to surpass her own teacher. Marble became less friendly and more aloof toward her presumptuous student.

Four months into the lessons, they clashed again. Marble called Billie Jean to tell her she wasn't feeling well. Instead of expressing sympathy, Billie Jean blurted out, "I guess that means I won't be coming up today." Marble chastised her pupil for her selfishness and hung up on her. When Billie Jean's parents called Marble to apologize for their daughter's rudeness, Marble told them Billie Jean would have to find a new teacher. Billie Jean never took another lesson from Marble and returned to being coached by Walker.

Billie Jean's game was improving to the point where she was selected to be part of the Junior Wightman Cup team in 1959 and 1960, when she was 15 and 16. The Wightman Cup is an annual competition, begun in 1923, between women from the United States and Great Britain. The Junior Cup is for young players.

Billie Jean was playing well enough to earn sponsorships to tournaments she'd missed out on the year before. She and the other teens on the women's circuit felt as footloose as college kids on their spring break. They stayed with families during their tennis tournaments but had plenty of time to make new friends and see the countryside they were passing through. Billie Jean remembers one particular stretch in Philadelphia where she must have gained 20 pounds eating ice cream. She also met some helpful tennis coaches as she traveled on the East Coast. One of them, Frank Brennan, offered to replace the cheap nylon on her racket with real gut, a thin tough string made from animal intestines.

Brennan invited Billie Jean to stay with his family whenever she traveled to New Jersey, and he hired her to work a few sessions at his tennis school. It was the first time Billie Jean had spent any length of time around people who talked about tennis at the dinner table. She learned a great deal about game strategy by listening to Brennan and absorbing his ideas.

By the middle of 1960, Billie Jean, 16, was the fourth-ranked woman in the United States. But if she had any notions about how good she was, the people around her were quick to put her in her place, just as Marble had done during their summer together. Brennan, whom she respected greatly for his knowledge and kindness, told her one day that she would be a great tennis player—not because she was a great athlete but because she was ugly, implying that she would devote herself to improving her game rather than wasting her time on boys, clothes, or makeup, the way prettier girls did.

Billie Jean was stunned by the comment and such a sexist attitude. But then, girl and boy tennis prospects were treated very differently. Billie Jean noticed how tennis pros such as Jack Kramer and Pancho Gonzales fawned over boys her age who showed potential but ignored girls like Karen Hantze and Billie Jean. Poten-tial female role models, such as Maureen Connolly, didn't pay Billie Jean the kind of attention she would have wished for ei-ther. Connolly, whom Billie

TENNIS PROS . . . FAWNED OVER BOYS HER AGE WHO SHOWED POTENTIAL BUT IGNORED GIRLS LIKE KAREN HANTZE AND BILLIE JEAN.

Jean admired greatly, took Billie Jean out to dinner one night after a tournament and asked her what her goals were. When Billie Jean told her she wanted to be num-ber one, Connolly called her self-centered and egotisti-cal and said that she would never be a champion.

Billie Jean didn't understand why Connolly would say such a thing. In 1953, Connolly had been the first woman to complete the Grand Slam—winning the Australian Open, the French Open, Wimbledon, and the U. S. Open all in the same year. She had been one of Billie Jean's idols as Billie Jean practiced ground strokes in the living room and worked her way up the ladder in junior tournaments. The comment made Billie Jean doubt herself for a time. But as her career continued to advance, she became even more convinced that she would prove her critics wrong.

Maureen Connolly won the Grand Slam in 1953. She was the first woman to accomplish that feat.

Billie Jean enjoyed some of her greatest moments at Wimbledon.

A Love Affair with Wimbledon

BILLIE JEAN HAD BEEN FASCINATED WITH WIM-
bledon for as along as she could remember. Wimbledon's All England Lawn Tennis and Croquet Club
has hosted the lawn tennis championships of the
world for men since 1877. It was the first international
tournament.

Tennis began as an indoor game in thirteenth-
century France. The original French game was called
Jeu de Palme, because it was played by batting the ball
with the palm of the hand. Rackets were added later.
In the fourteenth century, the British imported that
version of the game to the courtrooms of the wealthy
aristocracy. In 1874, Major Walter Clopton Wingfield
invented the outdoor version of the game, which continues to be played.

This color lithograph shows a tennis player in the early 1900s.

Once outdoor tennis was invented, it spread to the United States and throughout the world. Wimbledon added a women's tournament to the championships in 1884. The British dominated the women's singles and doubles championships at Wimbledon until the 1920s when Helen Wills Moody came onto the scene for the United States. From the late 1920s until the 1960s, American women ruled Wimbledon, winning 23 of the 27 tournaments held from 1927 to 1960.

By 1961, Wimbledon had become a legendary, almost mythic tournament for women players that showcased the games of such tennis greats as Suzanne Lenglen of France, Charlotte Cooper of England, and Moody, Alice Marble, and Maureen Connolly of the United States. Any player hoping to be considered number one in the world knew she must win there.

Daydreams can sometimes make the actual event seem anticlimactic. But for Billie Jean, seeing Wimbledon for the first time in June 1961, the setting was as inspiring as she had imagined it would be in her school essay as a 14-year-old. She had skipped her graduation ceremony at Long Beach Polytechnic High School to play in the most famous tennis tournament in the world.

Action during the 1900 women's tournament at Wimbledon

The day before play began, a British sportswriter, Gerry Williams, took her to see Centre Court, the grandstand-encircled court where the finals are played. Billie Jean was thrilled by the beauty of the green grass, the ivy that ran along the walls of the grandstand, and even the dark green of the grandstand seats. She noticed how the roof that sheltered the grandstand from rain made the place look like a theater, the tennis court its stage.

Billie Jean's doubles partner and her roommate for the tournament was Karen Hantze from San Diego. Hantze was ranked the number two player in the United States. Billie Jean was number four. They'd been traveling companions, as well as opponents, since the summer of 1959. Perry Jones had suggested they team up for doubles. Billie Jean and Karen found the same things funny. Both were impressed with the grandeur of Wimbledon, but they were not so awed that they would let it deter them from playing with their usual carefree abandon.

Still, Billie Jean was surprised when Hantze looked at the doubles pairings upon their arrival and announced, "I think we can win this." To save money, they had booked plane reservations that called for a return flight after the quarterfinals. Billie Jean hadn't packed a dress for the traditional Wimbledon Ball, figuring she'd wait until she was a champion to attend.

Billie Jean and Hantze won their first three doubles matches to make it to the finals against two tough

Australians, Margaret Smith and Jan Lehane. Each time the U. S. players won a match, they had to change the plane reservations to the next day. They were renting one of the small, dormitory-like rooms in London set aside for Wimbledon participants. When they first moved in, their landlady had treated them stiffly. But each day that they returned to their room victorious, the landlady became friendlier. By the time they reached the final, she was cooking them meals and calling them "my girls."

Billie Jean and Hantze proceeded to beat Smith and Lehane in straight sets to become the youngest pair

Teenagers Karen Hantze and Billie Jean Moffitt stunned Wimbledon by winning the doubles title in 1961.

ever to win the Wimbledon doubles title. When Bud
Collins, the tennis writer for *The Boston Globe,* found
out the winning doubles partners weren't going to the
Wimbledon Ball that night, he took them out for
spaghetti. After their victory meal, Billie Jean and
Hantze stayed up half the night, packing and giggling
and eating the rest of their store of candy bars.

When Billie Jean got home from Wimbledon, she
learned that Clyde Walker had died of cancer three
days after their Wimbledon victory. He had lived long
enough to hear about Billie Jean's triumph. His widow,
Louise, told Billie Jean how thrilled he was in the last
week of his life to read about her march through the
tournament to the doubles championship.

Billie Jean was thrilled to win in doubles, but she
knew the true measure of a tennis player was the singles tournament. She thought a great deal about that
goal, even as she put away her tennis racket for the
winter and commuted to Los Angeles State College, 18
miles from Long Beach.

Billie Jean had no idea what she wanted to major in,
but everyone else with half-decent grades was going to
college, so she figured she might as well, too. She liked
her classes and met many new friends. But she couldn't
wait for spring, when she would begin preparing for
her second trip to Wimbledon.

In 1962, Billie Jean and Hantze won the doubles
championship at Wimbledon again. In singles, Billie
Jean faced top-ranked Margaret Smith in a match on

Hantze and Billie Jean teamed up again in 1962 to successfully defend their Wimbledon doubles title.

Centre Court in the second round. Billie Jean lost the first set quickly, 6–1. But then the wind began to pick up, and Smith lost her rhythm and timing as she tried to adjust to the ball's haphazard flight over the net.

Billie Jean took the second set 6–3, but Smith regained her composure and went ahead 5–2 in the third and deciding set. Billie Jean then won the next four games to go ahead 6–5. With Billie Jean serving for the victory, crowds of people left the other courts and

Billie Jean and Margaret Smith walk off the court after Billie Jean's 1962 upset victory at Wimbledon.

jammed into the stands of Centre Court, hoping to see a major upset. When Billie Jean came to the net and swatted a backhand volley down the line for the winning point, the crowd broke into deafening applause. For the first time in the history of Wimbledon, the number one-ranked contestant had been defeated in her opening-round match. It was the beginning of an intense, sometimes bitter, rivalry between Billie Jean and Margaret Smith.

The next day's newspaper headlines hailed "Little Miss Moffitt, an ebullient bundle of energy and repartee." Billie Jean went on to lose in the quarterfinals. Her quest for a singles title would have to wait for another year.

That fall, as Billie Jean returned to Los Angeles State College for her sophomore year, she again hung up her tennis racket for the winter. She moved to an apartment near the school and got two part-time jobs to help pay her rent. One job was as a playground instructor near campus. The other was in the field house on campus, handing out towels and equipment to women on their way to gym class.

That fall, a friend introduced Billie Jean to a classmate named Larry King. The friend thought they would be a perfect match because they both liked tennis and neither of them smoked or drank. Billie Jean was a little stunned by the bright red socks Larry was wearing when he propped up his feet on the table where he was studying. But she thought Larry, with his baby face and blonde hair, was a handsome guy. For the next six months, they often studied across from each other at that table in the campus library. After classes, they met at the Inferno, a campus snack bar, where Billie Jean would order a hot fudge sundae and watch Larry play bridge.

Finally, in March 1963, they went out on their first date. The evening consisted of dinner at Billie Jean's parents' house and dancing at a club afterward. Within a month, Billie Jean and Larry were dating seriously. By the time she headed for Wimbledon in June 1963, Billie Jean thought she might be in love. Larry was sure.

"I was taken with her immediately," he said in a 1974 interview. "Within a few weeks, I just knew we would be married someday."

Larry never thought about dating other girls while Billie Jean was at Wimbledon. He worked in an ice-cream container plant to earn tuition money. He also changed his major from biochemistry to pre-law because Billie Jean said she wanted to marry a lawyer.

Billie Jean was not expected to go very far at Wimbledon that year. Smith was again seeded, or ranked, number one. They each advanced to the finals at Centre Court where Smith took her revenge by beating Billie Jean in straight sets. The press still considered Billie Jean an underdog. Her flashy style and chunky legs and torso didn't fit the British image of a proper Wimbledon champion. But Billie Jean had fully expected to defeat Smith for her first title. As Billie Jean walked off the court, she felt like a failure.

> HER FLASHY STYLE AND CHUNKY LEGS AND TORSO DIDN'T FIT THE BRITISH IMAGE OF A PROPER WIMBLEDON CHAMPION.

"Just remembering that day got me through a lot of tough matches in the next few years," Billie Jean recalled years later. "It wasn't a very good feeling and I didn't want to repeat it, ever."

By 1964, Billie Jean was considered one of the best women tennis players in the world. She had been a member of four winning Wightman Cup teams. She also had won her singles match in the first Federation Cup tournament in 1963, helping the United States defeat Australia. Twice during those years, Billie Jean was ranked number two in the United States. But number two wasn't good enough for her. And losing consistently to Smith made it even harder to bear.

She lost to Smith again in 1964, this time in the Wimbleton semifinals. So in September of that year, Billie Jean began to think about leaving California

Emotional and open, Billie Jean bemoans a mistake during the 1963 Wimbledon quarterfinals.

to spend three months in Australia improving her game. Billie Jean didn't worry about missing a semester of school. She was bored with her classes in history, her major, and she was getting only average grades.

Billie Jean and Larry were still dating. He proposed to her in a Long Beach coffee shop three weeks before Billie Jean was due to leave for Australia. Though he knew he would miss her, Larry agreed with Billie Jean that giving up her studies and becoming a year-round tennis player was the only way to break through to number one. Billie Jean barely had time to tell anyone about her engagement before she left.

In Australia, Billie Jean studied with Mervyn Rose, a former Australian tennis star. Rose had made a name for himself coaching young players, and Billie Jean's decision to study under him was a declaration that she wouldn't be satisfied until she was number one.

Rose completely revamped Billie Jean's serve to give her more power. He told her to throw the ball higher and farther out in front of her so that she'd really have to reach for the ball. This helped her hit the ball harder by compensating for the fact that she was only 5 feet 4 inches tall. But first, Billie Jean had to master the technique. At one point she was so out of synch that she lost a match to a 14-year-old girl and double-faulted 35 times.

Rose also changed Billie Jean's forehand, shortening her backswing to the point where she hardly had one at all. He told her to grip her racket tightly, keeping the racket head in front of her wrist instead of letting it droop behind her.

Rose's most important contributions to Billie Jean's development were his lessons in tennis strategy. As homework, Rose instructed Billie Jean to watch other people play and analyze each of their shots.

"When I went to bed at night, I was so tired and so confused by all this that my head felt like a basketball," Billie Jean recalled years later.

When she wasn't playing tennis, Billie Jean was sprinting, jogging, and missing Larry terribly. At night, despite her fatigue, she usually sat down and wrote him a letter before collapsing.

By the end of her three months in Australia, Billie Jean was no longer the chunky number-two player who could be worn down by a long match. She had

> WHEN I WENT TO BED AT NIGHT, I WAS SO TIRED AND SO CONFUSED BY ALL THIS THAT MY HEAD FELT LIKE A BASKETBALL.

the stamina to endure three sets every day. She also had the wisdom to accompany her improved physical skills.

The work didn't pay off instantly. She was eliminated again in the 1965 Wimbledon semifinals, this time by Brazilian Maria Bueno. But that fall, Billie Jean reached the U. S. Open final for the first time.

Billie Jean was ahead of Margaret Smith 5–3 in the first set of that final match, and she was ahead 40–15 in the next game, needing only one more point to win. But Smith came back to tie the set and eventually won it, 8–6. The same thing happened in the second set. Billie Jean went up 5–3, but Smith rallied to win the set and the match, 8–6, 7–5.

Billie Jean could have been more devastated by this loss than she'd been by her 1963 Wimbledon defeat. But as she stood beside the court during the trophy presentations, she realized that Smith had won because of something she herself was lacking: the killer instinct. Billie Jean lacked the ability to reach back and find the confidence and strength to put a match away on sheer will. She reasoned that if she could develop such confidence and single-minded determination, she could beat anyone in the world.

"It just came to me in a rush, as clear as a bell," she recalled later. "And suddenly the fact that I'd lost the match didn't bother me at all."

A few weeks after the U. S. Open, Billie Jean and Larry were married in Long Beach at the First Church of the Brethren, the church where she'd once told Bob Richards she would become a tennis star. On her wedding day, she carried a bouquet of roses and wore a long, white lace-trimmed gown and a matching veil. She and Larry spent part of their honeymoon at a tennis resort in Northern California so that she could continue to practice every day. Back home, they moved into an apartment not far from campus where Larry was still going to school and working the graveyard shift at the ice-cream carton factory. Billie Jean taught tennis on Saturday mornings to help make ends meet.

Billie Jean and Larry on their wedding day

She also continued to participate in amateur tournaments in Southern California. She figured she would play tennis for a few more years before settling down to raise a family.

The next time Billie Jean played Smith was in a South African tournament in April 1966. This time, Billie Jean displayed a more mature, determined attitude as she easily beat her rival, 6–3, 6–3. As she prepared for Wimbledon that June, Billie Jean felt that nothing could stop her from earning her first singles title there.

Billie Jean met Smith in the semifinals of Wimbledon in 1966, and she again defeated Smith easily. Her opponent in the finals would be another nemesis, Maria Bueno, who had beaten her the year before.

Bueno and Billie Jean were both crowd pleasers. Bueno's style was fluid and graceful while Billie Jean's was wilder and more aggressive. But Billie Jean knew that Bueno's smooth style hid one serious flaw: she was slow rushing the net after her serve.

As Billie Jean and Bueno left the dressing room beneath the grandstands and walked together to Centre Court where 15,000 spectators awaited them, Billie Jean had never felt so much tension or wanted to win so badly. She was not afraid, just anxious to begin.

The day was clear and windy, like the day she'd beaten Smith in her opening-round match five years before. The two players began cautiously. Billie Jean tried lobbing the ball to test Bueno's overhead returns. That strategy worked for the first set, which Billie Jean won easily. But Bueno began to feel comfortable with her overhead return and she put away enough of Billie Jean's lobs to earn the second set. The third set was grim and tense for Billie Jean, even though she only lost one game. As Bueno tired, she became even slower than usual following her serve to the net. Billie Jean returned a number of Bueno's serves hard, past

Bueno's approaching lunge, for winners. After winning match point, another passing shot that Bueno couldn't reach, Billie Jean threw her racket in the air as the crowd cheered her victory.

Billie Jean shook hands with Bueno and waited for the red carpet to be rolled out for Princess Marina, who was representing England's royal family at the tournament. Billie Jean curtsied to the princess and smiled broadly as she took the silver platter awarded the Wimbledon winner. Billie Jean felt happier than she'd ever felt before. Finally, she'd reached the goal she had worked toward since she was 10 years old.

Maria Bueno and Billie Jean hold the traditional flowers before their 1966 Wimbledon championship match.

Billie Jean's success at Wimbledon gave her a chance to speak out about unfair practices by tennis organizations.

FIGHTING FOR EQUALITY

BILLIE JEAN'S 1966 WIMBLEDON WIN SET THE stage for a banner year in 1967. Like a baseball player on a hot batting streak, she found everything about her game coming together at the same time. Larry took a week off from his factory job to go to Wimbledon with Billie Jean. He watched her win the singles title, as well as the doubles and mixed doubles tournaments.

Billie Jean also won her first U. S. Open singles title that fall, along with the doubles and the mixed doubles titles. She became the first woman to win singles, doubles, and mixed doubles at both Wimbledon and the U. S. Open in the same year since 1939—when Alice Marble had accomplished the feat. Billie Jean's victories ensured that she would be ranked number one in the world for 1967.

Winning the Wimbledon title put Billie Jean halfway to a Grand Slam in 1967. She defeated Ann Jones (at left) *of Great Britain.*

Billie Jean used her growing fame to begin speaking out against the hypocrisy of calling tennis players amateurs even though they were paid "under the table" for their appearances. During the 1960s, the top tennis players in the world were still considered amateurs. In sports, an amateur is a player who does not earn money for performance. Instead, the athlete's expenses are paid by the sponsoring government or sports association. Amateurs were thought to be "purer" athletes than those who earned their living in sports because they were making financial sacrifices for the love of their sport. In reality, amateurism created an unfair situation that favored the best-known players or those from the wealthiest families. Amateurs in all sports were routinely paid in cash behind the scenes by tournament directors who wanted them to appear in their tournaments. That meant that only those players invited to play—or those wealthy enough to pay their own expenses—could afford to consider a career in tennis.

Billie Jean called the practice "shamateurism." She urged the mighty United States Lawn Tennis Association to open its tournaments to all athletes. She predicted that if they did, most amateurs would turn professional. But the USLTA didn't want to change things. Officials were afraid that "open tennis," as it was called, would take tennis—and the profits from tournaments—away from the country clubs where the game had been played for decades and put it in the hands of players and promoters who wanted to make money for themselves.

Critics of open tennis also argued that professionalism would create athletes who didn't play for the love of the sport, but simply for the love of money. They also feared that open tennis would destroy the patriotic spirit that tennis players brought to the men's Davis Cup and the women's Federation Cup tournaments. In these single-elimination tournaments, teams of players representing a particular country play each other in singles and doubles, with the team winning the most matches advancing to the next round. If a country's best players could earn more money playing elsewhere, the critics argued, then the strength of the Davis and Federation Cup teams would be diluted or unbalanced, and victory would lose its meaning.

Billie Jean answered the critics every chance she could, even though USLTA officials threatened to suspend her for her comments. In those days, tennis tournaments had to be sanctioned by the tennis association, and only players deemed eligible by the association could enter them. Still, Billie Jean continued to use post-tournament press conferences as an excuse to rail against the system.

> I FEEL STRONGLY THAT TALENT OUGHT TO BE REWARDED AND SERVICES RENDERED OUGHT TO BE PAID FOR, NOT GIVEN AWAY.

"Nobody considers an amateur painter or an amateur writer or an amateur inventor more talented or dedicated than a professional," Billie Jean wrote in her first autobiography, echoing the ideas she repeated over and over again. "I feel strongly that talent ought to be rewarded and services rendered ought to be paid for, not given away."

Other well-known tennis players, such as Australians Rod Laver and Roy Emerson, also spoke out at this time. Arthur Ashe, the number-two ranked American at the time, told reporters, "We all deserve Oscars for impersonating amateurs."

In 1968, increasing public criticism from athletes slowly forced tennis associations in Great Britain and then the United States to end the hypocrisy of amateurism and open their tournaments to professionals. Players who had been paid for putting on exhibitions, coaching, or entering tournaments in which prize money was awarded were no longer excluded from the major tournaments, such as Wimbledon and the U. S. Open, that were still sponsored by national tennis associations.

The acceptance of professionalism led to corporate sponsors underwriting tournaments of their own. Tennis players—used to living on maybe $20,000 a year in expense money—had a chance to earn two or three times that much.

In April 1968, Billie Jean King and three other women became the first women professionals. Ann Jones, Françoise Durr, and Rosemary Casals felt as strongly about "shamateurism" as Billie Jean did. That year, they were each paid $40,000 to join the National Tennis League, a league formed by George McCall, a former Davis Cup champion turned promoter. Along with the four women, the league included six men: Pancho Gonzales, Rod Laver, Ken Rosewall, Andres Gimeno, Fred Stolle, and Roy Emerson.

Billie Jean recalls the league's first spring as a series of one-night stands played in out-of-the-way places. The strangest place was a small town in the Po Valley of Italy where they played one night on a freshly laid

Rosemary Casals (left) *Billie Jean, and Françoise Durr, along with Ann Jones, became the first women tennis professionals.*

asphalt court lit by incandescent light bulbs strung up on poles. The new tar stained the soles of their sneakers and their tennis balls were black after a few games. In the dim lighting, they could hardly see to return the ball on the court.

The new professionalism was good for tennis because it brought the game to people and places that had never had a chance to witness matches before. But the tour was "bloody murder" on Billie Jean and her fellow pros, she said.

"We always seemed to finish playing around 2 A.M., rarely got to sleep until 4, and then we had to get up at 6 in order to arrive at the airport at 7," she recalled. "By the end of it, I wouldn't have cared if I died."

Billie Jean and her fellow professionals took time out from the new National Tennis League events to enter the traditional tournaments, such as Wimbledon, that were open to professionals for the first time. In 1968, Billie Jean felt a lot of pressure at Wimbledon, not only to win her third title in a row, but also to prove that professional tennis, with its increased number of events, wasn't undermining the quality of play in these traditional events.

Billie Jean's parents made their first trip to Wimbledon in 1968 to see her play. Billie Jean was glad to have them there to support her. The British press,

After turning pro in 1968, Billie Jean went to Wimbledon determined to win her third title in a row.

which had made her their darling after her first, and even her second win in 1967, had switched to rooting for new underdogs to beat her. Billie Jean was also struggling with increasing pain in her left knee, which had bothered her off and on for the past few years.

Billie Jean faced Ann Jones in the semifinals. Billie Jean lost the first set to Jones and was in danger of losing the second set and the match. Behind 5–3, she rallied to win the second set. She won the third set easily to advance to the final.

Her final match with Judy Tegart was another long battle that Billie Jean won, 9–7, 7–5. As soon as she arrived back home in the United States, Billie Jean had her left knee operated on and she spent the last six months of 1968 recovering.

By January 1969, she was back on the road with the National Tennis League. She took a break from the professional tour in June 1969 for Wimbledon, where she hoped to win her fourth singles title in a row. In the final, she faced Ann Jones, whom she had defeated in that long, three-set semifinal match the year before. The British fans' sympathy for Jones, who had been to Wimbledon 13 times and never won, was obvious. The crowds that had once cheered Billie Jean's shots and crowded Centre Court to catch a glimpse of her only politely clapped at her winning points. Billie Jean noticed the shift and felt almost betrayed by it. "They'd go through the motions and applaud a good shot of mine, but they did it in such a blatantly cool way that

I knew that what they really wanted was for me to dump the ball into the net," Billie Jean wrote of that year's Wimbledon.

Billie Jean also felt the linesmen and lineswomen were against her. She was beaten by Jones in three long sets to break her three-year string.

> **I KNEW THAT WHAT THEY REALLY WANTED WAS FOR ME TO DUMP THE BALL INTO THE NET.**

The partisan crowd got inside Billie Jean's head that day, but she had other things on her mind as well. She and Larry had been arguing before the match. The subject of their disagreement soon was forgotten, but it was a sign of the changes going on in their marriage.

Larry had finished law school, passed his bar exam, and joined a law firm in Hawaii, where the pace was slower and the weather even nicer than in California. Because of the move, Larry and Billie Jean were seeing less of each other than they ever had. While he took time off occasionally to watch Billie Jean play, Larry was bored hanging around a hotel room alone while she practiced. Because of Billie Jean's busy schedule, she was only home for three months out of the year, and then for only five or six days at a time. During these times, Billie Jean got tired of sitting on the beach while Larry worked. She didn't enjoy cocktail parties and the social scene that went along with being a lawyer's wife. She also hated the extra hours she spent

Billie Jean and Larry worked at their long-distance marriage.

flying from Hawaii back to the mainland whenever she had a tournament.

Larry left his law practice in 1970 and moved back to California to become a tennis promoter and Billie Jean's business manager. Yet this new arrangement didn't increase their time together. Larry would be in one city promoting a tournament while Billie Jean was in another city playing. They both realized they were drifting apart, but they didn't even have time to talk about it. For the time being, they accepted the way things were as the price they had to pay for their success. They hoped that after Billie Jean retired, they could have a more conventional marriage.

Yet Billie Jean also feared that might never happen. Though she loved Larry and considered him to be her best friend, she had begun to admit to herself that she was attracted to women. The feelings frightened and confused her, and she certainly wasn't ready to talk about them or act on them. She was afraid of what would happen if her family—and the public—found out.

"I was starting to become so visible," she recalled of that time in a 1998 interview in *Women's Sports & Fitness* magazine. "There was just this terrible fear of being ostracized."

By 1970, so many tennis players had decided to turn professional that the USLTA and other tennis associations realized they had better start awarding prize money if they wanted the top players to enter their tournaments. "Shamatuerism" was officially dead. The sport was growing, and prize money was being offered from all directions. The problem was, the men running most of the sanctioned tournaments didn't want to share the new prize money equally between men and women. So while most tournaments traditionally had featured both a men's and a women's championship, a number of tournaments started dropping their women's divisions. Within a year, the International Lawn Tennis Association was sanctioning 15 tournaments for men only, tournaments that previously had included women.

The big tournaments, like Wimbledon and the U. S. Open, had too much history to exclude women. Billie

Jean met Margaret Smith, who had begun using her married name, Margaret Court, yet again in the 1970 final at Wimbledon. Billie Jean had the advantage over Court three times in the first set, 6–5, 7–6, and 8–7. But she could never finish her off. Court went on to win in two sets, 14–12, 11–9. It was the longest women's final in Wimbledon history.

Billie Jean had her right knee operated on that summer and didn't compete in the 1970 U. S. Open that fall. But she attended the tournament in Forest Hills and became embroiled in the ongoing debate over unequal prize money for women.

All the women at Forest Hills were talking about Jack Kramer, the organizer of the Pacific Southwest Tournament, a major event in the United States that would take place a few weeks after the U. S. Open. Kramer had set the prize money for the men's winner at $12,500. Meanwhile, all eight female quarterfinalists had to share a pot of prize money that added up to only $7,500. The woman who won got $2,000 of that.

Furious at the disparity, Billie Jean asked Gladys Heldman, the founder, publisher, and editor of *World Tennis Magazine,* to talk to Kramer about the prize money. But Kramer, one of the pros who had fawned over male prospects but ignored the females when Billie Jean was a kid, wouldn't budge. He was an old-fashioned, ex-tennis player himself who believed that the women's game, with its longer rallies and slower serves, was inferior to the men's style of play. He was convinced that tennis fans would much rather see men play than women, even though women such as Billie Jean and Margaret Court were as well known as any male player.

While the women players fumed, Heldman used her position as magazine publisher to generate change. She decided to sponsor a tournament just for women in Houston the same week as the Pacific Southwest Tournament. The USLTA, bowing to pressure from Kramer, refused to sanction the tournament and threatened to suspend any woman who played in it. If suspended, a

Billie Jean defeated Virginia Wade before losing to Margaret Court in the 1970 Wimbledon tournament.

Gladys Heldman was Billie Jean's ally as the two fought for fair treatment of women tennis players.

woman would be unable to enter the prestigious USLTA events like the U. S. Open the following year.

To get around that issue, Heldman came up with the idea of having the women players become contract professionals paid by *World Tennis Magazine.* That way, the tournament wouldn't need sanctioning. She also got Joseph Cullman, chairman of the Philip Morris company, to help sponsor the tournament and award the winner $7,500. This first event was such a success that Cullman agreed to help sponsor a series of tournaments.

Thus, the Virginia Slims tennis circuit for women was born. The tour was named after the brand of longer, leaner cigarettes that the company was marketing solely to women. The Virginia Slims advertising slogan was "You've come a long way, baby," a slogan that was often applied to the tennis tour as well. Sixteen women risked their careers and signed on to play in 14 tournaments beginning in January 1971.

The USLTA suspended Billie Jean and all the women who played in the Houston tournament but grudgingly reinstated them a few weeks later. The International Lawn Tennis Association, which governed international tennis, also initially banned the players on the Slims tour but accepted them back when they realized they needed names like Billie Jean King to attract fans to their tournaments.

The women's tour quickly grew into a successful venture, but not without hard work on and off the court. Like the National Tennis League Billie Jean had belonged to in 1968 and 1969, the women's tour brought women's tennis to out-of-the-way stadiums and arenas in big and small cities across the country. Everywhere the tour stopped, the players would do television interviews, sell tickets, and circulate among the crowd to sign autographs. The Slims tour caught the eye of Bobby Riggs, a former Davis Cup player and the 1939 Wimbledon champion. In his 50s, Riggs had earned a reputation as a hustler, a guy who played tennis against anyone who would put up money to play. Riggs challenged Billie Jean to a match for $5,000. But Billie Jean felt she had nothing to gain by playing him. If she won, people would say, big deal. If she lost, she feared people would believe the men who were making disparaging remarks about the women's tour, saying women's tennis had no right to demand the same money, TV time, or press coverage as men.

A few women players, such as Court, refused to support the new Virginia Slims tour. Court's decision wasn't because the tour's sponsor was a cigarette company marketing its product solely to women. In 1971, few people thought about the relationship between smoking and cancer or heart disease, even though

> BILLIE JEAN FELT SHE HAD NOTHING TO GAIN BY PLAYING RIGGS. IF SHE WON, PEOPLE WOULD SAY, BIG DEAL.

the Surgeon General of the United States had begun warning of the health hazards of smoking in 1964. Virginia Slims executives had promised not to advertise in such a way that teens would be enticed to smoke.

Court's objections had to do with her family. She preferred to play in mixed tournaments, where her husband, Barry Court, who traveled with her, was more likely to have some male companionship. Court also hated tennis politics and considered herself a traditionalist. It would irritate her when Billie Jean would mention Court as an example of a modern, independent woman. Court would criticize Billie Jean for being so outspoken, off and on the court.

Billie Jean played in 13 of the 14 Virginia Slims tournaments in 1971, earning $37,000 through her eight tournament wins. The money put her over the $100,000 mark for the year, making her the first woman athlete ever to earn that much money. However, Billie Jean lost to Evonne Goolagong, a young Australian player, in the semifinals at Wimbledon that June. Neither Goolagong nor up-and-coming star Chris Evert had signed on with the Virginia Slims tour, preferring to wait and see how the new circuit fared before committing themselves.

Evert—blonde, blue-eyed, petite, and only 16—was garnering headlines for her stellar play and her attractiveness. She hadn't lost a singles match since Wimbledon, and she was being touted as the greatest thing to come along in women's tennis since Maureen Connolly won her first title in 1951 at the age of 17.

The fans loved to watch Chrissy play, and their partisan cheering seemed to paralyze her opponents in the first two rounds of the 1971 U. S. Open. Billie Jean was slated to play Evert in the semifinals. While she wasn't nervous about the partisan crowd, she was fearful of the message that another loss to a young tennis star would send about her and the Virginia Slims tour.

"How could we claim that we had the best talent and that our circuit was the future of women's tennis if our best player—me—was going around getting knocked off by a couple of teenagers," she wondered as she warmed up for the match. "For a few minutes, I panicked. I wanted to run, to do anything but walk on that court and play that match. But finally I said, 'My God, Billie Jean, you've got to get a hold of yourself. It can't end here, not now.'"

The crowd went wild when Evert came back from
0–40 to win the first game of the first set. But Billie
Jean was confident of her game plan. She continued to
change the pace of every serve and return, giving Evert
no chance to get into a rhythm against her. In the sev-
enth game, with the score tied 3–3, the "Little Ice
Maiden," as Evert was called, finally cracked. She
double-faulted and then lost a long rally when Billie
Jean broke off a perfect drop shot to make it 0–30.
Billie Jean went on to break Evert's serve and win the
next two games to take the set, 6–3. She easily took
the second set, 6–2.

The final against Rosie Casals was almost anticlimactic. Billie Jean beat Casals in straight sets for her
second U. S. Open singles title. She proved that at the
age of 27 she was still the woman to beat in women's
tennis and that the Virginia Slims circuit had the best
players in the world on its tour.

Sports Illustrated put Billie Jean King on its cover
as sportswoman of the year because of all her achievements. The 20-year-old magazine had never before
honored a woman in this way. Billie Jean was being
touted as a role model for young girls interested in
sports and women fighting for equal pay in the workplace. What the public didn't know was that in 1971
Billie Jean had also become a role model for those
women fighting for the right to choose abortion.

In February 1971, Billie Jean had discovered she
was pregnant. She went back to California to tell

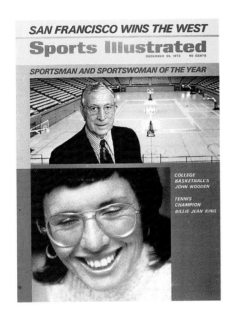

SAN FRANCISCO WINS THE WEST

Sports Illustrated

DECEMBER 25, 1972   60 CENTS

SPORTSMAN AND SPORTSWOMAN OF THE YEAR

COLLEGE
BASKETBALL'S
JOHN WOODEN

TENNIS
CHAMPION
BILLIE JEAN KING

Sports Illustrated *magazine honored Billie Jean as its Sportswoman of the Year in 1972. UCLA men's basketball coach John Wooden was the Sportsman of the Year.*

Larry. Abortions were illegal in 1971, but many doctors would perform them for patients who could afford to pay. Billie Jean and Larry talked over the problems in their marriage and the goals they wanted to achieve. They agreed that they weren't ready to start a family.

"I was so unclear about everything," Billie Jean said in a 1998 interview. "At that moment in my life, I was totally overwhelmed with my sexuality, my homophobia. Now, looking back, knowing what I know about myself—how much I like kids—I would have said to Larry . . . 'I'm going to have this kid. You and I maybe shouldn't be together, but I can take care of the kid myself.' But I always thought a kid needed a father."

Billie Jean felt strongly that she was making the right decision, but she kept the abortion a secret from most people, including her parents. She knew her parents would be upset. They had already started talking about wanting grandchildren. A few players on the tour knew about the abortion, but none of the newspaper reporters who covered tennis asked her about it. In 1971, the press was much less apt to write about a celebrity's personal life. What an athlete did off the court only became important if it led to an injury or landed them in jail.

Billie Jean inadvertently gave the press an excuse to write about her abortion in early 1972 when she agreed to add her name to a petition advocating abortion rights. The petition appeared in an advertisement in *Ms.* magazine. Billie Jean didn't realize the headline over the list of names would read: "We have had abortions." She thought she was admitting only to supporting a woman's right to choose.

Billie Jean was defensive when reporters began asking her whether she had really had an abortion. She hedged at first, knowing her parents would read the headlines. She wanted to discuss the issue with them first. But a reporter for *The Washington Post* wrote a story in February 1972 that told when and where Billie Jean had undergone her abortion. Billie Jean was appalled, but she began answering questions.

Billie Jean talked to her parents on the phone a week or so after the news broke but no one mentioned the abortion. They finally talked about it on Mother's Day, when Billie Jean and Larry visited her parents. Betty Moffitt told her daughter that she had cried for three days when she read about the abortion in the newspaper. She said she trusted Billie Jean, though she didn't understand her decision.

Billie Jean received lots of hate mail, most of it unsigned. She also heard from women who praised her honesty and said her example made them less ashamed of their own choice to have an abortion. Those letters buoyed her spirits and gave her the confidence to continue speaking out on women's issues.

In 1972, Billie Jean campaigned on behalf of Title IX, legislation requiring schools that received federal funding to provide equal sports programs for boys and girls. The controversial bill was debated fiercely by women and men seeking greater opportunities for their daughters and by athletic directors who didn't want to share scarce resources with women. Billie Jean testified before Congress about her own experiences growing up. She told the representatives that increased opportunities for girls would help bridge the performance gap between men and women in many sports. Her testimony helped persuade lawmakers to pass the bill, which was signed into law by President Richard Nixon in the summer of 1972.

In 1972, Billie Jean defeated Evonne Goolagong at Wimbledon, won the U. S. Open and the French Open but missed the Grand Slam because she skipped the Australian Open to play on the professional tour. In 1973, she beat Bobby Riggs.

BATTLE OF
THE SEXES

IN JUNE 1972, BILLIE JEAN WON AT WIMBLEDON again, avenging her 1971 loss to Evonne Goolagong, the Australian teenager who had beaten her in the semifinals the year before. That spring she also won her first French Open, and in the fall, she capped things off with her second straight win in the U. S. Open by defeating Kerry Melville. But the Grand Slam of tennis—winning the four major tournaments in the same year—continued to elude her. She had failed to enter the Australian Open because of her commitment to the Virginia Slims tour.

Still, as 1973 began, Billie Jean King was the biggest name in women's sports since Babe Didrikson Zaharias, who had captured the hearts of Americans in the 1940s and '50s with her exploits on the golf course.

Billie Jean once again won the Wimbledon title in 1972 after a three-year drought.

Billie Jean had her name on a Wilson-brand tennis racket and was endorsing products in magazines and on television. She also spearheaded the drive early that year to create the Women's Tennis Association, a union of women professionals who together could lobby for more equitable prize money in the big-name tournaments such as Wimbledon.

It came as no surprise when Bobby Riggs called another press conference early that year to renew his challenge to Billie Jean to play him. Billie Jean kept turning Riggs down. But when Riggs played and beat Margaret Court 6–2, 6–1 in a May 1973 match dubbed the "Mother's Day Massacre," Billie Jean could not ignore him any longer. Court, who stood for everything traditional in women's tennis and was critical of women's liberation, had agreed to play Riggs. But she was not prepared for the media attention that surrounded the match. Court seemed inept and overmatched against Riggs. She had viewed the event as little more than an exhibition, a way to make some easy money—a guaranteed $10,000, win or lose.

Billie Jean was in an airport terminal in Hawaii on the way home from Japan when she heard about Court's loss. As she listened to the radio account of how easily Riggs had beaten Court, Billie Jean got more and more agitated. Fellow tennis player Rosie Casals and Marilyn Barnett, a hairdresser whom Billie

Marilyn Barnett (left) *was Billie Jean's hairdresser and personal assistant in the early 1970s.*

Jean had hired to be her personal assistant a few months before, tried to calm her down. Yet they knew by the look in Billie Jean's eyes that she had decided she had no choice but to play Riggs.

In 1973, plenty of people still believed that women didn't deserve equal money—that watching a women's match didn't compare to watching the men. Putting her reputation on the line by playing a 55-year-old man still seemed reckless but after Court's defeat, Billie Jean felt she had to take the risk. "It's pretty scary to remember the way people thought back then. Like women always choke. They belong at home. People really believed that," recalled Billie Jean 20 years later. "I did it to prove that women could walk and chew gum at the same time. To keep pushing that philosophy that women need equal opportunity."

> I DID IT TO PROVE THAT WOMEN COULD WALK AND CHEW GUM AT THE SAME TIME.

Before she made her final decision, Billie Jean called Larry to get his advice. Billie Jean and Larry were as busy and had as little time to see each other as they had in 1971 and 1972. Their San Francisco apartment had become a storage space where they hung their clothes and kept some belongings. An unopened bottle of champagne was the only thing in their refrigerator. Yet Larry and Billie Jean talked almost every day. Larry was against the idea of Billie Jean playing Riggs.

"I didn't think it would be good for her," he told reporters. "There was so little to prove that would be positive for women."

As her manager, Larry knew the match would be good publicity. And he knew Billie Jean felt compelled to play. In June, Billie Jean defeated Chris Evert for her fifth Wimbledon singles title. She and Rosie Casals also teamed up for their fifth Wimbledon doubles championship, Billie Jean's ninth Wimbledon doubles title. Soon after Wimbledon, Billie Jean announced that she would play Riggs. Immediately, the hype over the

Chris Evert, an attractive teenager, challenged Billie Jean's hold as America's favorite. Here, the two are shown waiting out a rain delay at the 1973 Wimbledon tournament.

"Battle of the Sexes" began with the mischievous Riggs fueling a lot of it.

"Women belong in the bedroom and the kitchen," the 1939 Wimbledon champ said over and over again, to anyone who would listen. Riggs's antics reminded many of Muhammad Ali before a big boxing match.

"Here he was all of a sudden the celebrity he'd never been when he was the best tennis player in the world back in 1939," said Bud Collins, who was covering tennis for *The Boston Globe.* "It was like he'd been in a time capsule and been rediscovered. He was fun, lively, eminently quotable. It was terrific for him and for everybody."

Indeed, the media was having a grand time turning the match into a metaphor for the changes going on in society at large. In 1973, more and more women were joining the workforce. The women's movement had its own magazine in *Ms.* While good old boys like Riggs were saying women belonged at home, not in the workplace, a song by Helen Reddy, "I Am Woman," was number one on popular music charts. And Billie Jean—who the year before had admitted to having had an abortion and who lobbied publicly for Title IX— had become the patron saint of many women struggling to assert themselves at work, on the playing fields, or at home.

All summer long, the upcoming match was a topic of conversation in grocery stores, local bars, and beauty salons. Husbands and wives argued over the dinner table about who would win, just as vehemently as senators on Capitol Hill debated whether Richard Nixon was involved in the growing Watergate scandal. Bella Abzug, a Congresswoman from New York and an ardent feminist known for her colorful hats, made bets with half a dozen colleagues in the halls of the House of Representatives—not on Nixon's impeachment, but on Billie Jean beating Riggs.

The prematch hype gained momentum in the three weeks preceding the big event. Stanford University's marching band formed the letters B-J-K as it played Reddy's "I Am Woman" during halftime of the Stanford-Penn State football game shown on national TV. An elderly woman came up to Billie Jean at a supermarket and told her, "I hope you beat his pompous ass." The sports editor at *The Boston Globe* had told Collins in early September not to bother going to Houston for the match. A few days later, he came up to Collins and said, "Gosh, you'd better go."

Meanwhile, Billie Jean had other tennis matches to play. Two weeks before the match with Riggs, she was scheduled to play in New York at the U. S. Open, the tennis circuit's premier American event. Billie Jean finally had succeeded in getting tournament promoters to make the prize money for men and women equal. She was excited about that feat as well as the prospect of winning her third straight U. S. Open. No woman had done that since Maureen Connolly in 1953.

After getting through the first two rounds, Billie

Bobby Riggs was a hustler, and he turned his exhibition match against Billie Jean into a nationwide event.

Jean drew Julie Heldman, a player who was good at changing pace and upsetting her opponent's rhythm. Billie Jean was fighting a sore throat and a fever when she took the court. The early September day was humid and hot—the kind of weather in which Billie Jean usually played well. But she felt woozy the minute she stood up to start the match. Billie Jean gutted out a 6–3 win in the first set. By the second, though, the sky had started spinning and her racket felt like a six-ton weight.

"I don't remember much after the first set except thinking, 'Hold on, just hold on. If you get through this match, everything will be all right,'" she recalled.

The problem was, Heldman played deliberately, using every minute allotted to her between serves and sets. During net changes, after every two games, she would fidget with her racket and retie her sneakers—anything to keep Billie Jean waiting. Billie Jean didn't know how long she could endure the stalling tactics. After Billie Jean lost the second set and fell behind 4–1 in the third, she slowed down, too. She sat and toweled herself off during net changes and took long, deep breaths before she served. But while Billie Jean had suffered in silence at Heldman's delaying tactics, Heldman loudly complained about the time Billie Jean was taking during and between games. Finally, Billie Jean said, "If you want the match that badly, you can have it." She walked off, forfeiting the match.

Sportswriters began to speculate that all the hype and attention leading up to the Riggs match was getting to Billie Jean. Could a woman handle such relentless pressure? *Newsweek* editors were planning to put Billie Jean on their cover the week before the Riggs match but decided against it after she pulled out of the Open, fearing the Houston match would be canceled.

Billie Jean blamed her undoing on a virus. She was sick when she played and lost to Chris Evert in an exhibition match in North Carolina. Perhaps all the pressure did contribute to Billie Jean's short temper and her illness. But she was going to make sure that if Riggs beat her, it would be because he was the better tennis player.

For the two months before she faced Riggs, Billie Jean had begun spending time alone every day in quiet meditation to prepare her mind for the match. She also began lifting weights to strengthen her legs, especially her knees. After a brief rest to recover from the virus, she returned to this training regimen for the final week leading up to the match.

Billie Jean had accepted Riggs's challenge to play a three-out-of-five-set match, instead of the customary two-out-of-three that the women played. "I said to myself, 'That's fine macho boy, let's see how you do,'" she told a reporter years later. "I had trained hard. I could have gone 10 sets."

The week before the match with Riggs, Billie Jean traveled to Hilton Head in South Carolina to spend a few days with Pete Collins, the resident pro. She and Collins practiced together for two hours a day during those few days at Hilton Head. They worked especially hard on her volleying and her overhead returns. She knew Riggs would try to lift as many lobs as he could and hope that she would lose a few in the Astrodome lights. To practice, she returned as many as 200 lobs a day to Collins.

> I SAID TO MYSELF, 'THAT'S FINE MACHO BOY, LET'S SEE HOW YOU DO.'

Billie Jean and Collins watched films again of the Court-Riggs match to discover Riggs's weaknesses. Though they were bitter rivals, Billie Jean called Court and asked her for advice on how to beat Riggs. Billie Jean, her assistant, and Dick Butera, a business associate, left Hilton Head and flew to Houston the Sunday night before the match. Larry had flown in earlier and had a hotel suite waiting for them and for Billie Jean's parents, who flew in on Monday from Long Beach.

In the final days before the match, Billie Jean hit for two hours a day with Dennis Van der Meer, her game coach. Billie Jean changed her sleeping habits, forcing herself to stay up late and sleep until 10 or 11 A.M., so that she would be at peak, midafternoon form when she stepped onto the court at 8 P.M. for the match.

"I really didn't know if I'd win," Billie Jean has said. "But I was going to do everything in my power to win by working out, just by being totally organized and ready. I was in great shape."

Billie Jean was also intent on having things go her way off the court. ABC Television had hired three announcers for the broadcast: Howard Cosell for the play-by-play and Rosie Casals and Jack Kramer for color commentary. About a month before the match, Billie Jean had warned Roone Arledge, the head of ABC Sports, that she would not play if Kramer were one of the broadcasters. Kramer had been openly scornful of women's tennis and had refused to raise the women's prize money for his tournament in 1971. Billie Jean had also had personal run-ins with him during tournaments. With such bad blood between them, Billie Jean had no desire to give Kramer a chance to degrade women's tennis or gain publicity for his own tennis ventures.

Arledge may have figured that having Kramer and Casals in the same broadcast booth would be great theater—another battle of the sexes to match the one being played on the Astrodome floor. Two days before the match, Kramer was still scheduled to appear.

In the bold style that won her many friends and enemies during those pioneering years, Billie Jean met with Arledge the day before the match. She told the network executive that she would walk off the court if Kramer was in the booth that night. Arledge tried to change Billie Jean's mind but she wouldn't budge, despite the money at stake. After several hours, Arledge agreed to replace Kramer with Gene Scott, a player on the men's tour. Billie Jean had won the first big point.

Finally, Thursday, September 20, 1973, the day of the match arrived. Willie Mays, the legendary baseball player, chose that day to announce his retirement after 22 years. The first supersonic Concorde to visit the United States landed in Dallas to help dedicate the Texas city's new airport. Yet those news events were all but lost amid the excitement of the King-Riggs match. *The New York Times* previewed the match as if it were a prize fight, comparing the height, weight, chest, wrist, biceps, neck, forearm, hip, and thigh measurements of the two competitors.

Las Vegas oddsmakers had announced a line on the match, and the gambling was frantic in the hours preceding it. Most of the money was being bet on Riggs. "I can't find a dime's worth of King money in town," crowed Riggs to reporters the night before the match. Bud Collins, who didn't bet on the match, predicted a Riggs victory on a sports talk show. Riggs held court in his hotel room until 2 or 3 A.M., telling anyone who'd listen why he was favored to win.

"This is my cup of tea, my dish, this pressure, this circus stuff," he told Grace Lichtenstein, a reporter for *The New York Times.* "I don't believe with the eyes of the world upon her that she's as stable as I am."

> I DON'T BELIEVE WITH THE EYES OF THE WORLD UPON HER THAT SHE'S AS STABLE AS I AM.

Bobby Riggs loved the publicity and hoopla surrounding his challenge to Billie Jean.

Billie Jean spent the afternoon before the match in her hotel room dancing to the soundtrack of *Jesus Christ Superstar*, listening to the music of her friend Elton John, and eating candy bars. She used the mellow songs to steady her nerves and the upbeat numbers to energize and focus herself, as she had for most big matches. Still, she was so nervous she couldn't keep her feet still. Around 4 P.M., she went over to the Astrodome and walked out onto the field. The tennis court had been stretched out over a plywood basketball floor. It was raised on a platform and surrounded by yellow folding chairs, like a boxing ring. The glassed-in broadcast booth sat at one end of the court. A champagne bar and a carving-board cart for sliced roast beef were set up at either end. A red carpet was laid out from the court to the entranceway where Riggs and Billie Jean would come in and greet the 30,000 fans waiting for them.

Billie Jean did an interview with ABC Sports, then ventured onto the court to hit some balls with Dennis Van der Meer. The playing surface was slow all over and dead in some spots, like a basketball court. She figured that would take some getting used to.

Billie Jean drank some Gatorade and ate another candy bar. Then she began to pace around the visitors' dressing room at the Astrodome. A trainer pointed out the cubicle that Billie Jean's brother, Randy, used when the San Francisco Giants were in town to play the Houston baseball team. For several minutes she

Billie Jean's little brother, Randy, pitched for the San Francisco Giants.

stood by the cubicle and thought about her brother. He was a steady relief pitcher for the Giants, among the league leaders in saves and earned-run average. She was as proud of him as he was of her. She thought, too, about her mother and father. They had sacrificed so much to help their children realize their dreams. Then she thought about her career and the importance of the match with Riggs.

"It really came home to me hard that if I lost to Riggs, much of what we'd won for ourselves might go right out the window," she said. "Everybody else was having a ball in Houston but that hour before Bobby and I actually stepped onto the court was probably the most agonizing of my life."

The festivities surrounding the King vs. Riggs match were unlike those for any other tennis match—ever.

Eight o'clock was showtime. The scene had none of the staid, dignified air of any previous lawn tennis match. Billie Jean had always hoped to bring tennis to the masses, and on this night she did. Bands played, balloons rose to the rafters, and the crowd whistled and cheered "Right on, Billie Jean" as she appeared in a gold litter held up by four toga-clad Rice University male track stars. Billie Jean wore a wool cardigan sweater over a white tennis dress trimmed in blue brocade and rhinestones. She had on blue suede sneakers and a blue sweat band. Smiling weakly, she waved one hand in the air to the crowd. She clenched the other hand in her lap as she fought a bad case of butterflies from prematch jitters and her fear of heights.

Then Riggs, looking like a bespectacled leprechaun as he basked in the spotlight, was wheeled out in a rickshaw pulled by six professional models in tight red and gold outfits. They were Bobby's "bosom buddies," the women he'd hired to trail him around everywhere in the week before the match.

Once he alighted, Riggs presented Billie Jean with a gigantic Sugar Daddy. She gave him a live piglet—a male chauvinist piglet, she told him—she had named Larimore Hustle. Larimore was Riggs's middle name. The pig got lost in the excitement of the match but was later found curled up in a corner of the stadium.

Billie Jean won the coin toss and elected to serve. She couldn't believe the noise of the crowd as the match began. She also couldn't believe Riggs was so slow getting to the ball to return her serves. As they changed sides after she won the first game, she said to Van der Meer, "He's putting me on, right?"

But Riggs wasn't being coy. Billie Jean's strategy was working. She mixed up her serves, slowing them down so he could not counterpunch against her power. She concentrated on hitting to his backhand—which Court had told her was his weakness—and made him reach for shots whenever she could.

"When we changed sides at 2–1, I thought my chances were good," Billie Jean recalled. "He was hyperventilating and really nervous. I was nervous, too, but I had it under control better than he did so I knew that was going to be a factor."

Still Riggs, his shirt drenched with sweat, hung in there. He went up 3–2 with Billie Jean serving when she missed a backhand volley by a couple of inches. The crowd let out a groan as Billie Jean's racket drooped at her side and she shook her shoulder-length brunette hair. As they changed sides again, Billie Jean thought how crucial this next game would be. If Riggs held his serve and won, Billie Jean would have to win four out of the next six games. But if she broke his serve, the momentum would shift back to her.

Billie Jean decided that she'd been too careful with her shots, trying to place them in the corners to make Riggs cover more ground and wear him out. Instead, she would just hit the ball boldly and charge the net when she could. She won two of the next three games to even things at 4–4. Many of the points in those games were long ones that ran Riggs ragged but seemed to energize Billie Jean. On one crowd-pleasing point, she ran down a ball hit wide and deep to her forehand. When Riggs returned it wide and deep to her backhand, she ran that one down, too, scooping the second shot up into a baseline lob that gave her time to get back on the balls of her feet. She then slashed Riggs's weak return into the corner beyond his reach.

The first set ended with Riggs failing to serve in-bounds twice in a row—a double-fault. Billie Jean won 6–4. Of the 34 points she won in the 10 games, 26 had been on shots Riggs never touched.

"The long points seemed to wilt him," recalled Rosie Casals. In the ABC broadcast booth, she correctly predicted the final scores of each set early into the match.

Billie Jean lost while serving in the first game of the second set. But once again, she coolly regained her composure and the momentum. She broke Riggs's serve in the second game with her favorite shot—a running backhand that she drove crosscourt. When Riggs returned her serves,

> WHEN RIGGS RETURNED HER SERVES, BILLIE JEAN FIRED BACK WITH HARD, LOW GROUND STROKES THAT HE COULD NOT REACH. BILLIE JEAN WENT ON TO WIN FIVE OF THE NEXT SEVEN GAMES TO TAKE THE SET **6-3.**

Billie Jean fired back with hard, low ground strokes that he could not reach. Billie Jean went on to win five of the next seven games to take the set 6–3.

By the third set, Riggs had changed shirts and was noticeably slower. Billie Jean took a 2–0 lead, but she began to feel cramps in her lower legs. Riggs won the next two games to make it 2–2. Billie Jean turned around and won the next two games, breaking his serve at 40–0 in the sixth game. At that point, Riggs stopped play and went to the sidelines to have the cramps in his hands massaged. No one knew that Billie Jean was trying to ignore pain in both of her legs.

Riggs returned to the court and won the next game on Billie Jean's errors to cut her lead to 4–3. She won her serve in the next game to make it 5–3. The final game was tied 40–40 five times before Riggs double-faulted to give her match point. The crowd streamed onto the court when Riggs sent a high backhand volley into the net to end the match. Billie Jean threw her racket into the air and pumped a victory fist as Riggs jumped the net to congratulate her. "You're too good," he said as he draped an arm around her shoulders. Her game face dissolved into a wide smile. "I just felt relief. I remember thinking, 'Thank God it's over,'" recalled Billie Jean. "I think he underestimated me."

Boxer George Foreman was supposed to present Billie Jean with the $100,000 check at courtside when the match ended. But he couldn't get to her because of

Billie Jean quickly wore down the older Bobby Riggs.

After losing, Riggs jumped the net and went to congratulate Billie Jean.

the crush of well-wishers and spectators. With Larry on one side and Marilyn Barnett on the other, they pushed Billie Jean through the crowd to the sideline. Larry lifted his wife up onto a table so she could wave her trophy at the crowd and blow them kisses. Foreman finally found his way to Billie Jean with the check. She remembers looking down at all the zeroes after the one and thinking she'd never seen that much money before.

About 40 million people had watched the match on TV. All over the country, people cheered their television sets as if they were in the Astrodome.

"On campuses, women were hanging out of dorm windows cheering," recalled Gloria Steinem, founder of *Ms.* magazine. The *Ms.* staff turned into a raucous group of women in the magazine's Manhattan office as Billie Jean cruised to victory.

"It was sort of like Jackie Robinson for women," added Steinem. "It was terribly, terribly important."

Indeed, the match was an energizing moment for many women athletes, young and old. The day after the match, a group of women reporters at the *Philadelphia Bulletin* walked into their editor's office and demanded to be paid the same as the men on the staff. Billie Jean received hundreds of congratulatory

George Foreman, who was then the heavyweight boxing champion, presents Billie Jean with the winner's check.

telegrams, but the one that tickled her most was from a girls high school basketball team in Oklahoma that praised her for giving girls more of a chance to compete in sports.

In the months after the match, women athletes slowly began to get more coverage in newspapers and magazines, and on television. In the year following the match with Riggs, Billie Jean was profiled by *Good Housekeeping, Ladies' Home Journal,* and *Seventeen.* The articles gushed about this tomboy turned tennis star. *Esquire* ran a profile of Billie Jean in which the male author said that he found her athletic style "sexy."

The victory legitimized women's tennis and gave the sport a boost. Billie Jean, the daughter of a fireman and a housewife in California, proved that an athlete didn't have to belong to a country club to excel at tennis. Tennis courts became fixtures in playgrounds all over America. School boards voted to add girls' and boys' tennis to their extracurricular activities.

Billie Jean showed thousands of people that women athletes were enthralling, steely competitors even under the glare of a spotlight they seldom faced. "We had an unbelievable forum. It was visual and physical," Billie Jean said 20 years later. "I knew then it would always be the thing people remember most about me because of the exposure. I'd put it near the top of women's sports achievements." Yet in 1973, Billie Jean's greatest personal challenges still lay ahead. Her pioneering days were far from over.

Billie Jean started the Women's Sports Foundation with the help of other prominent female athletes, including Martina Navratilova.

RETIRING TOO SOON

BILLIE JEAN'S VICTORY OVER BOBBY RIGGS MADE her an international celebrity. She used her new-found fame to gain sponsors and attention for her growing business ventures, which included *womenSports,* a magazine devoted exclusively to sports for women and girls. Billie Jean also was a founding member of the Women's Sports Foundation, an organization devoted to expanding opportunities for women and girls in sports through grants, research, events, and activities that increased the awareness and visibility of women in sports.

Another venture Billie Jean and Larry worked on was World Team Tennis, a league of 16 teams of professional men and women tennis players who played against each other in cities such as Boston, New York,

Philadelphia, and Los Angeles. She and Larry helped found the league and were the major financial backers, along with businessmen such as Dick Butera, who owned the Philadelphia team. The late 1960s and the 1970s signaled a new era in the world of sports. World Team Tennis was just one of many sports ventures designed to take advantage of the public's growing interest in sports and television's growing appetite for sports events. New leagues were started in basketball, hockey, and football, as well as in soccer and women's basketball.

The idea behind Team Tennis, which Billie Jean promoted all through her career, was to bring tennis to the general public and to show kids that men and women could compete together toward a goal in sports. During matches, teams competed against each other in men's singles and doubles, women's singles and doubles, and mixed doubles.

In 1974, Billie Jean was the player-coach for one of the teams, the Philadelphia Freedom. Her friend, singer Elton John, wrote a song about the team that year. Billie Jean was paid $100,000 for the season, which extended from early spring to late summer. Attendance went up wherever her team played.

Team tennis was scored differently than regular tennis. Individual games did not have to be won by two points. If the players got to 40–40, the next point decided the game. If a set went to 6–all, a nine-point tiebreak would decide the set. The changes made for a faster-paced, more exciting game to watch. Fans of World Team Tennis were encouraged to shout, wave signs, and cheer as if they were attending a baseball game instead of a tennis match. Some players were unnerved by catcalls while they were serving. But Billie Jean, who earned the nickname "Mother Freedom," proclaimed that this was tennis the way she liked it.

"They didn't pay their money to come and whisper to themselves all night," she said in her autobiography, published that year. "Let 'em scream and shout is the way I feel about it."

Like professional soccer leagues and women's basketball leagues in the 1970s, World Team Tennis didn't capture much media attention or television coverage in its first year. But several thousand fans in each of the cities where it was played supported the teams. A smaller version of the league continues to exist.

In the meantime, Billie Jean also played on the international tennis circuit. In 1974, Olga Morozova, a Russian, beat Billie Jean in the quarterfinals of Wimbledon. Billie Jean lost her composure over a line judge's call and proceeded to smash a ball over the grandstand in disgust. Her angry act prompted a horrified murmur from the crowd, followed by a heckler shouting, "You're a bad sport."

Billie Jean was really more frustrated with herself than with the line judge. Her serve was tentative, and she was missing her usually reliable backhand volleys. She didn't want to blame it on her right knee—

the knee on which she'd had surgery twice in the past five years. But the pain was constant and distracting.

Billie Jean went into the U. S. Open that fall hoping to redeem herself. The singles final pitted Billie Jean against Evonne Goolagong, who was 22 and at the top of her game. Goolagong had beaten Billie Jean in 1971 at Wimbledon, but since then, Billie Jean seldom had lost to the Australian, despite the fact that Goolagong played her best on grass.

Billie Jean could adjust her game to play on grass, clay, or the synthetic surfaces of the indoor arenas of World Team Tennis. She could win a game from the baseline if she had to, or she could beat her opponent coming to the net if the situation called for that. When respiratory problems had begun to bother her in her middle 20s, she learned how to pace herself, summoning the stamina she needed for a long, tough match.

Billie Jean lost the first set 3–6 but came back to win the second 6–3. The third set was one of the finest ever played at Forest Hills. Goolagong went ahead 3–0, but she couldn't hold her serve the rest of the way and Billie Jean battled back. Using her backhand volley, a shot that some tennis writers called the best in the game, male or female, Billie Jean rushed to the net time and again to hit shots past Goolagong's reach. Billie Jean had the crowd buzzing as she dived to her knees and stretched seemingly beyond her reach to return Goolagong's shots. From that 3–0 deficit, she came back to win the third and final set 7–5.

Another Billie Jean first was the creation of womenSports, *a magazine geared to athletic women and their interests.*

Despite, or maybe because of, this achievement, Billie Jean began to think about retiring. Many athletes continue playing long after their skills have begun to decline, sometimes just for the money they can earn by simply showing up. Larry told Billie Jean she was crazy to consider retiring. But Billie Jean said she didn't want to be remembered as a has-been.

*Billie Jean celebrates
her fourth U.S. Open
championship.*

As 1975 approached, Billie Jean decided to make that year's Wimbledon her final singles tournament. She planned to continue in doubles, hoping to reach 20 wins at Wimbledon—a feat that would break the record set 30 years before by Elizabeth Ryan.

Although Billie Jean and Rosie Casals had won five Wimbledon doubles titles together, Billie Jean thought a change would prolong her doubles career. Billie Jean's new doubles partner, Martina Navratilova, was a young player from Czechoslovakia. Navratilova confided in Billie Jean that she was secretly preparing to defect to the United States.

Billie Jean announced her plan to retire and prepared for Wimbledon in 1975 with the zeal she had brought to her match with Bobby Riggs three years earlier. The result was a "near perfect match," she told the press afterward. She defeated Chris Evert in the semifinals and then Evonne Goolagong (using her married name, Cawley) 6–0, 6–1 in the final for her sixth Wimbledon title in 15 tries. The final match was much easier than her U. S.

I'M NEVER COMING BACK.

Open final match had been. She proclaimed that, at the age of 32, she was glad her singles career was over.

"I'm never coming back," she told reporters.

Within a year, Billie Jean began to reconsider. She had enjoyed the first few months of her retirement. She found it fun to stay up late and be able to eat ice cream again without worrying about ruining her training. She even enjoyed relaxing on the beach. Billie Jean had once hoped that her retirement would bring her and Larry closer, but she realized it was too late for that. He was busier than he'd ever been and she was still as confused about her sexuality as she had been 10 years earlier.

"I didn't know who the hell I was," she remembered in a 1998 interview.

Billie Jean also was gaining weight. She had been a junk food binge eater since her teens, but the rigor of the tennis tour had helped her stay in shape. Without an outlet for her physical and emotional energy, candy bars and ice cream were taking their toll.

She also began to miss the excitement of playing tennis on a world stage—in front of thousands of tennis fans—with no one to blame but herself for the outcome of the match. She decided to have her knee operated on for a third time. If the surgery went well, she told herself, she would make a comeback in singles.

The surgery went smoothly, but the doctors told Billie Jean it would take her a year to regain top form. She didn't listen. She worked out at fitness gyms and weight training rooms before it was common for women to do so. She hoped to build up her leg strength so that her knee would be less susceptible to the constant twisting and turning of tennis than it had been in the past.

Sometimes when she worked out, Billie Jean saw Arthur Ashe, the first black man ever to win at Wimbledon. He, too, was trying to rehabilitate his career. Billie Jean had been critical of Ashe in the past for not supporting women's efforts to equalize prize money. But as they compared notes and boosted each other's spirits, they realized they had a lot in common. He had been a pioneer as a black man in a predominantly white sport. She was a pioneer for all women's sports.

Less than six months after her surgery, Billie Jean

made her return to Wimbledon, where she lost to Chris Evert in the quarterfinals of the 1977 tournament. Just being there was enough for Billie Jean.

"Maybe I can be happy being number eight instead of number one," she told a reporter after the tournament. "At this stage, just playing, that's winning enough for me."

In 1978, Billie Jean won no major tournaments in singles or doubles. That year was not a good one for World Team Tennis either. Some of the owners decided to quit because the league was still losing money. Billie Jean and Larry pleaded with them to give the league more time to mature. Attendance had grown from 1,700 per match to 5,700 per match in the previous five years, and the league's losses were down from $10 million to $1 million a year. But without a major television network broadcasting their events on a regular basis, the other owners didn't think the league could survive.

MAYBE I CAN BE HAPPY BEING NUMBER EIGHT INSTEAD OF NUMBER ONE.

In 1979, Billie Jean got back into the headlines by breaking the record for Wimbledon titles when she and Martina Navratilova took the doubles crown. It was a poignant moment for Billie Jean. The woman with whom she had shared the record, Elizabeth Ryan, passed away the day before the match at age 88. A few months before her death, Ryan had been asked how

*Billie Jean and Martina Navratilova joined forces to win the 1979
Wimbledon doubles title for Billie Jean's record-setting 20th title.*

she felt about someone breaking her record. She
replied that if the record had to go, she hoped Billie
Jean would break it.

Ryan's death made Billie Jean realize that her own
career, as remarkable as it was, would someday be sur-
passed by someone. "People who make records push
you up to a different level," Billie Jean told reporters
that day. "Twenty titles is a new standard, but you
know sometime, someone is going to break it."

Billie Jean's only win in international competition in 1980 was in the doubles tournament at the U. S. Open that fall. Once again she teamed with Martina Navratilova, as she had at Wimbledon in 1979. After the Open victory, Navratilova decided she wanted a new doubles partner. She never came right out and told Billie Jean that. Instead, she just started playing with Pam Shriver. Billie Jean had changed doubles partners several times over the course of her career. But she still was hurt, especially since she'd been such a friend to Navratilova over the years. Billie Jean confronted her the following spring. "Tell me I'm too old, . . . but tell me something," she begged Navratilova, but Navratilova wouldn't talk about it.

In 1981, Billie Jean, who was 37, thought about quitting tennis because of her knees. But that year, just before Wimbledon, Billie Jean's former assistant, Marilyn Barnett, filed a lawsuit against Billie Jean. The lawsuit claimed that Billie Jean and Barnett had been lovers. Barnett was suing to keep Billie Jean's house in Malibu, where she and Billie Jean had spent time together.

At first, Billie Jean denied Barnett's claims. But faced with the evidence of more than a hundred letters she'd written to Barnett over the years, Billie Jean decided to call a press conference. She admitted that she had had an affair with Barnett that began in 1972. Billie Jean called the affair a mistake because she was married, and she said it had been over for at least four years. She blamed it on the stress of living on the road

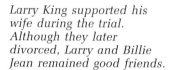

Larry King supported his wife during the trial. Although they later divorced, Larry and Billie Jean remained good friends.

for months at a time and the problems in her marriage. Larry was beside her as she sat at the microphone and fielded reporters' questions. He assured Billie Jean that they would somehow get through this crisis together.

Billie Jean's family also rallied around her. Her father was an old-fashioned man who made his negative feelings about homosexuality clear. But Billie Jean was his daughter. Retired, he continued to attend her tennis matches and cheered as loudly as ever. He would offer to get his daughter's autograph for young fans with whom he struck up conversations in the stands.

Billie Jean was afraid that Randy, still pitching for the San Francisco Giants, would be subjected to snide remarks and ridicule from teammates and fans. But Randy assured her that his teammates were giving him pats on the back and not criticism.

In need of income to fight Barnett's lawsuit, Billie Jean decided once again to postpone her retirement. Continuing to play would take some courage, she knew. She would have to weather the scandal in public and continue to answer questions from the media while she was trying to concentrate on tennis. But she used the opportunity to answer critics who said her admission proved that women's tennis was a breeding ground for homosexuality.

Billie Jean wrote her second autobiography in part to explain how she and Barnett had come to be lovers and to show that their affair was not a sign of rampant lesbianism in tennis. She said they had met when Billie Jean went to Barnett's beauty salon to have her hair cut. Over time, she said, they became friends and confidants. She blamed the affair on her loneliness. While Larry was unwilling and unable to give up his career to follow Billie Jean around the world, Barnett gladly did. When the affair ended, Billie Jean said that Barnett remained attached to her and wouldn't leave her house. While Barnett claimed that Billie Jean had promised her the house, the judge who heard the case found no merit in Barnett's claims.

Billie Jean received thousands of letters from people who told her that, once again, her courage had made life easier for them. Still, the damage to Billie Jean's financial situation was enormous. Admitting to a homosexual relationship can still make headlines, but it is far less perilous to one's career than it was in 1981.

Because of her admission, Billie Jean lost close to $1.5 million in endorsements over the next three years, including a $500,000 deal on a line of tennis clothing. While NBC continued to use her as a commentator on its tennis broadcasts, she knew that any corporations considering her to endorse products, or any charities wishing her to be a spokeswoman for them, would begin to think twice about their choice.

Billie Jean reached the semifinals of Wimbledon in both 1982 and 1983. Other players were beginning to wear the logos of their sponsors on their clothes, rackets, wrist bands, and even socks. But Billie Jean played on Centre Court for the final time in 1983 in

Billie Jean interviews Chris Evert during the 1983 U.S. Open.

an unadorned white dress with no one's logo on it. The scandal had indeed cost her sponsors.

Billie Jean's playing career began to wind down in 1984, after she reached the age of 40. She continued to play in smaller tournaments throughout the United States to help attract more fans to the game. She also competed in the senior division of tournaments such as the U. S. Open and became commissioner of a revived and revised version of World Team Tennis.

While they remained friends, Billie Jean and Larry decided to get a divorce in 1987 so that he could remarry and start a family. Billie Jean is the godmother of Larry's oldest son.

Billie Jean began to come to terms with her feelings for women after the divorce. She still was not willing to admit to her family or the world that her affair in the 1970s was part of an ongoing struggle to understand her sexuality. While she was courageous and open in so many areas of her life, Billie Jean's upbringing and the social taboos against homosexuality were still too strong for her to even consider making her sexual preference public. She began a long-term relationship with a woman a few years younger than she. But she refused to grant personal interviews or acknowledge that they were more than friends.

Billie Jean was elected to the Tennis Hall of Fame in 1987. As the 1980s came to a close, Billie Jean was beginning to find herself in as much demand as she ever had been as a tennis player.

After she retired from playing, Billie Jean found that she was also good at coaching. She enjoyed the new challenge.

LIFE AFTER TENNIS

WITH BILLIE JEAN AT THE HELM, WORLD TEAM Tennis became a more grassroots, recreational league in the late 1980s. The professional league was scaled down from the 16 teams that played all summer long in 1974 to an 8-team league that played for four weeks every September, with a league championship in December. A team still consisted of two men, two women and a coach. Among those who have played are Martina Navratilova, John McEnroe, Zina Garrison Jackson, and Lindsay Davenport.

The new recreational components of World Team Tennis included a junior version of Billie Jean's coed team concept for kids 18 years old and younger in more than a hundred cities and towns. Billie Jean and other professionals also began conducting clinics around the country for boys and girls interested in playing coed tennis.

Billie Jean enjoyed her executive role with World Team Tennis, but like any former, top-ranked athlete, her thirst for competition wasn't quenched by this venture. Only the thrill of the big tennis events— Wimbledon, the U. S. Open, the international circuit— could do that. So Billie Jean jumped back into competitive tennis as a special coach and consultant to some of the top players. Her first pupil was her former doubles partner, Martina Navratilova.

Navratilova had been the dominant player of the 1980s, winning the singles title at Wimbledon eight times. But by 1989, her career was in shambles. She hadn't won a Grand Slam tournament in two years and Steffi Graf had replaced her as the number one woman tennis player in the world. Navratilova had no idea what was wrong with her game. She was thinking of retiring when her coach, Craig Kardon, called Billie Jean. He hoped she could persuade Navratilova to stay in tennis by working with her on the things that were wrong with her game.

Billie Jean had long ago forgiven Martina for dumping her as a doubles partner. Still, Billie Jean knew that helping Navratilova rejuvenate her career might threaten her own Wimbledon record of 20 wins in singles, doubles, and mixed doubles. But Billie Jean realized her glory years were over. She also knew she would gain a measure of satisfaction by helping someone else attain the same heights she had.

Billie Jean persuaded Navratilova to give tennis a second chance by making her realize that she still had a lot to learn. Much of Navratilova's early success was due to her size and her strength. But as she got older and younger players came on the scene with as much endurance and strength as she had, Navratilova needed different match strategies, and she needed to better understand the fundamentals of each shot.

Over the next two years, Billie Jean and Navratilova spent many hours together breaking down each of Navratilova's shots. Billie Jean taught her student a new way of serving, just as Mervyn Rose had taught Billie Jean so many years before in Australia.

Billie Jean also worked on Navratilova's confidence. For all her success, Navratilova was plagued with self-doubt that could overcome her and cause her to lose focus in the middle of a tight match. Navratilova needed to learn to control her emotions on the court and channel them into her play—as Billie Jean herself had. Billie Jean told Navratilova to keep a diary, each day recording her ambitions in the past tense. That way, she told her pupil, they would become a self-fulfilling prophecy. The diary was also a place to write down her fears, insecurities, and observations—a place, Billie Jean said, to confront her emotions rather than hide from them. "It's about learning your craft," Billie Jean said. "I don't think it's so much about becoming a tennis player. It's about becoming a person."

Billie Jean sometimes teases her tennis players.

Billie Jean's coaching helped Navratilova to win her record ninth Wimbledon singles title in 1990. She credited Billie Jean with helping to restore her love for the game.

Billie Jean's newfound career drew some media attention when she took on her first male student, 30-year-old Tim Mayotte. Unlike Navratilova, Mayotte had never been a top-ranked player. He was always losing in the quarterfinals of a tournament, never reaching his potential. When he approached Billie Jean in 1990 about helping him out, she told him he would have to completely revamp his serve. She changed his serve and his whole demeanor on the court. From a reserved, self-conscious player, he became a more emotional, self-confident one. To loosen him up during practice, Billie Jean would sing the Elvis Presley song, "Please Release Me," to him from across the net. She gave him a five-dollar bill one day when he angrily smashed his racket into the ground after a missed shot.

Billie Jean answered skeptics who said a woman couldn't coach a man by pointing out that women may be more suited to be good coaches than men because girls are brought up to listen, to share, to observe, and to worry about others. "That makes us very nurturing," Billie Jean told *Women's Sports & Fitness* in 1992. "Men . . . often just want to take care of their own egos."

In the early 1990s, Billie Jean became involved in a business venture that has since become well known—Discovery Zone play centers for toddlers and school-aged kids. Billie Jean is co-owner of several franchises in California, where the concept began. In these play centers, boys and girls climb tall, padded blocks, crawl through long, winding chutes, slide down rollered ramps, and wade through ponds of plastic balls in enclosed areas. The centers are popular places on rainy days and for birthday parties. After an hour or two of play, kids are sweaty, thirsty, happy, and, presumably, a little more fit. The concept fits Billie Jean's belief that boys and girls should play and build their muscles together.

"If you and I have similar experiences growing up, we'll always understand each other," she explained. "We'll bond better and yes, boys and girls will compete. Life is competition."

Meanwhile, Billie Jean's success coaching Navratilova and Mayotte drew the notice of Les Snyder, president of the United States Tennis Association (formerly the USLTA). Billie Jean and the tennis organization had had a chilly relationship since the 1970s, when Billie Jean fought to equalize men's and women's tournament prize money. She still considered the USTA a sluggish,

Twenty years after the original "Battle of the Sexes," Billie Jean and Bobby Riggs joined forces to raise money for AIDS research.

Billie Jean coached the 1998 Federation Cup team from the United States, which included such stars as Monica Seles (second from left) *and Mary Joe Fernandez* (second from right).

traditional organization that had no use for free thinkers like herself. But Snyder reached out to Billie Jean in the early 1990s, believing tennis could benefit from her expertise as well as her pioneering image. He also felt the USTA owed Billie Jean a great debt because she'd been so instrumental in popularizing tennis. He felt it was time to mend fences.

"She wasn't being included in tennis and I thought this was the perfect place for her," Snyder said.

Billie Jean liked the idea of being involved with the Federation Cup, the international tournament she had participated in throughout much of her career. But she said she wouldn't work with the U. S. Federation Cup team unless the members wanted her. She called each of the players to discuss her coaching philosophy. The players, including top-ranked U. S. women Gigi and Mary Joe Fernandez and Lindsay Davenport, urged her to sign on as coach and to stay with the team for the 1996 Olympics in Atlanta.

Billie Jean was a tough taskmaster at times. She suspended Gigi Fernandez from the team for disruptive behavior. But she was fair, asking for the players' opinions before making most decisions about practice time and match pairings.

Billie Jean's Federation Cup team won the international championship in 1996. She was also credited with motivating Lindsay Davenport to improve her game enough to win the gold medal at the Olympics. Up to that point, Davenport, like Mayotte, had not achieved her potential. "She helped Lindsay believe in herself," said Snyder. "She's a tremendous motivator and she worked out a great relationship with the team."

Beyond strategy and skill development, under Billie Jean the Federation Cup players learned, as had Mayotte and Navratilova, how much fun it could be to rekindle their passion for the game of tennis. Billie Jean learned things, too, most important the value of patience and of treating each player as an individual.

"I had to judge when to take chances and when to back off," she said. "Sometimes being a cheerleader is good, sometimes you have to step back."

In 1995, just into her 50s, Billie Jean decided to deal with her ongoing problems with food. She checked into a residential treatment clinic in Philadelphia that is devoted to eating disorders. There, she came to realize that her eating problems were connected to her shame and her fears about her sexuality. She invited her parents to the center where she finally admitted to them, after years of hiding, that she was gay and that the woman she shares her high-rise Chicago condominium with is her longtime partner. Billie Jean says that the time in which she grew up made dealing

> BILLIE JEAN SAYS SHE FEELS MORE AT PEACE WITH HERSELF THAN SHE EVER HAS.

with her sexuality the hardest thing she's ever done. She feels more at peace with herself, she says, than she ever has.

In 1990, *Life* magazine had named Billie Jean one of the 100 most important Americans of the twentieth century. The only other athletes named to this impressive list were Babe Ruth, Muhammad Ali, and Jackie Robinson. Billie Jean not only revolutionized tennis but also pioneered changes that have led to mushrooming opportunities and achievements in women's sports. Only 300,000 girls in the United States played sports in 1971. More than 2.25 million girls were participating in high school sports by 1996. The 1996 Olympics in Atlanta showcased the first generation of girls who had been born and brought up with the benefits and opportunities required by Title IX. At those Olympics, female athletes from the United States won gold medals in swimming, gymnastics, track and field, basketball, soccer, softball, and—with Billie Jean coaching—tennis.

Since she was a teenager, Billie Jean King has been in the forefront of change, in tennis and in society. She admits that it's been a lonely life at times, but when asked in 1991 what she would list as her occupation, Billie Jean said she liked the sound of "pioneer."

Billie Jean signs her name below her footprints at her induction into the Tennis Hall of Fame.

S O U R C E S

10 Sally Jenkins, "Racket Science," *Sports Illustrated* (April 29, 1991).

12 Billie Jean King with Kim Chapin, *Billie Jean,* (New York: Harper and Row, 1974), 25.

13 Ibid., 27.

15 Ibid., 31.

21 Ibid., 34.

22 Ibid., 39.

24 Ibid., 37.

32 Ibid., 41.

38 Larry King, "My Wife, Billie Jean King, by her Husband," *Ladies' Home Journal,* (April 1974), 93.

38 King, *Billie Jean,* 73.

41 Ibid., 53.

42 Ibid., 58.

50 Ibid., 79.

50 Ibid., 82.

52 Ibid., 87.

54–55 Ibid., 95.

57 Anne Taylor Fleming, "The Battles of Billie Jean King," *Women's Sports & Fitness,* (September/October 1998), 134.

64 King, *Billie Jean,* 112.

65 "The Battles of Billie Jean King," 168.

72 Interview with author, September 1993.

73 "My Wife, Billie Jean King, by her Husband," 93.

74 Grace Lichtenstein, *A Long Way Baby,* (New York: William Morrow and Company, 1974), 22.

74 Interview with author, September 1993.

76 Interview with author, September 1993.

76 King, *Billie Jean,* 172.

77 Ibid., 172.

78 Billie Jean King with Cynthia Starr, *We Have Come A Long Way, The Story of Women's Tennis,* (New York: Regina Ryan Publishing Enterprises, Inc., 1988).

79 Interview with author, September 1993.

81 Lichtenstein, *A Long Way Baby,* 31.

83 King, *Billie Jean,* 180–181.

85 Ibid., 182.

85 Interview with author, September 1993.

87 Interview with author, September 1993.

88 King, *Billie Jean,* 184.

88 Interview with author, September 1993.

90 Interview with author, September 1993.

91 Interview with author, September 1993.

95 King, *Billie Jean,* 15.

95 The New York Times News Service, "Billie Jean Loses to Morozova." *The New York Times,* (July 4, 1974), 11.

99 United Press International, "A Sixth Wimbledon Crown," *Portland (Maine) Press Herald,* (July 5, 1975).

99 United Press International, "Billie Jean Happy It's Over," *Portland (Maine) Press Herald,* (July 5, 1975).

99 "The Battles of Billie Jean King," 168.

101 Tony Kornheiser, "King, Ashe

Want That Old Feeling
Again," *The New York Times,*
(November 27, 1977).

102 United Press International,
"King Sets Mark," *Portland
(Maine) Press Herald,* (July 8,
1979).

103 Billie Jean King with Frank
Deford, *Billie Jean,* (New York:
Viking Press, 1982), 193.

111 "Racket Science," .

113 Joel Drucker, "The Once and
Future King," *Women's Sports
& Fitness,* (November/
December 1992), 78.

114 Ibid., 79.

115 Interview with author,
September 1997.

116 Interview with author,
September 1997.

116 Sandra Harwitt, "U. S.
Scorches Australia," *Tennis*
(July 1995), 124.

B I B L I O G R A P H Y

Books

Blue, Adrianne. *Martina: The Lives and Times of Martina Navratilova.* New York: Birch Lane Press, 1995.

Court, Margaret Smith. *Court on Court.* New York: Dodd, Mead and Company, 1975.

King, Billie Jean, with Kim Chapin. *Billie Jean.* New York: Harper and Row, 1974.

King, Billie Jean, with Frank Deford. *Billie Jean.* New York: Viking Press, 1982.

King, Billie Jean, with Kim Chapin. *Tennis to Win.* New York: Harper and Row, 1970.

King, Billie Jean, with Cynthia Starr. *We Have Come A Long Way, The Story of Women's Tennis.* New York: Regina Ryan Publishing Enterprises, Inc., 1988.

Lichtenstein, Grace. *A Long Way, Baby.* New York: William Morrow and Company, 1974.

Marble, Alice, with Dale Leatherman. *Courting Danger.* New York: St. Martin's Press, 1991.

Articles

Amdur, Neil. "Discussed and Dissected, Billie Jean and Bobby Ready." *The New York Times,* September 20, 1973, 57.

Amdur, Neil. "Mrs. King Defeats Riggs, Amid A Circus Atmosphere." *The New York Times,* September 21, 1973, 1, 18.

Anderson, Dave. "The Professor." *The New York Times,*
September 21, 1973, 18.

Bodo, Peter. "The Best Event Nobody's Ever Seen." *Tennis,*
December 1996, 20–21.

Drucker, Joel. "The Once and Future King." *Women's
Sports & Fitness,* November/December 1992, 78–79.

Fleming, Anne Taylor. "The Battles of Billie Jean King."
Women's Sports & Fitness, September/October 1998,
131–134, 168, 171.

Harwitt, Sandra. "U. S. Scorches Australia." *Tennis,* July
1995, 124.

Jares, Joe. "Battle of the Ages." *Sports Illustrated,*
September 16, 1974, 22–25.

Jenkins, Sally. "Racket Science." *Sports Illustrated,* April
29, 1991, 66–78.

Keese, Parton. "Billie Jean King: An Attitude, Instinct and
Sense of Urgency." *The New York Times,* January 14,
1976, 45–46.

King, Larry. "My Wife, Billie Jean King, by her Husband."
Ladies' Home Journal, April 1974, 93.

Kornheiser, Tony. "King, Ashe Want That Old Feeling
Again." *The New York Times,* November 27, 1977.

Lichtenstein, Grace. "King-Riggs Match Point is Money."
The New York Times, September 19, 1973, 49, 58.

Lichtenstein, Grace. "Mrs. King Calls Victory 'Culmination'
of Career." *The New York Times,* September 21, 1973,
19.

Lobsenz, Norman. "The Winning Style of Billie Jean King." *Good Housekeeping,* March 1974, 88-89, 144–149.

Moffitt, Betty. "My Daughter, Billie Jean King, by her Mother." *Ladies' Home Journal,* April 1974, 92.

Nelson, Mariah Burton. "Billie Jean Talks Team Tennis." *Women's Sports & Fitness,* July, 1985, 15–16.

The New York Times News Service. "Billie Jean Loses to Morozova." *The New York Times,* July 4, 1974, 11.

United Press International. "A Sixth Wimbledon Crown." *Portland (Maine) Press Herald,* July 5, 1975.

United Press International. "Billie Jean Happy It's Over." *Portland (Maine) Press Herald,* July 5, 1975.

United Press International. "Evert Wipes Out Billie Jean's Return." *Portland (Maine) Press Herald,* June 28, 1977, 21.

United Press International. "King Sets Mark." *Portland (Maine) Press Herald,* July 8, 1979.

Wakefield, D. "My Love Affair with Billie Jean King." *Esquire,* October, 1974, 136-139.

Weir, Tom. "King Triumph Monumental 20 Years Later." *USA Today,* September 20, 1993, C1-2.

Wind, Herbert Warren. "Golddiggers of 1974." *The New Yorker,* October 7, 1974, 140-146.

Interviews with Billie Jean King, Bud Collins, Rosemary Casals, Gloria Steinem, and Les Snyder.

A NOTE ABOUT SCORING

The server calls out the score before each game, giving his or her score first. Zero is called love, the first point is 15, the second is 30, the third is 40 and the fourth is game. A player must score at least four points and have two more points than his or her opponent to win a game. When the score is tied at 40–40, the score is called deuce. Then a player must win two points in a row to win the game. When the server scores a point, the score is ad-in. When the receiving player is ahead, the score is ad-out.

A player must win six games and at least two games more than his or her opponent to win a set. When a set is tied at six games apiece, the players play a tie-break of 12 points. The first player to win 7 points and at least two more than his or her opponent wins the tie-break and the set.

Matches can be best-of-three, in which the first player to win two sets wins, or best-of-five, in which the first player to win three sets wins.

PHOTO ACKNOWLEDGMENTS

Photographs are used with the permission of: © ALLSPORT USA: pp. 1, 88, (Gary M. Prior) pp. 2-3, (USOC) p. 22, (MSI) p. 53; Corbis-Bettmann, pp. 2, 27, 31, 98; private collection of Billie Jean King, pp. 6, 8, 9, 16, 43; Seth Poppel Yearbook Archives, p. 15; Archive Photos: pp. 24, 36, 45, 48, 71, 73, (Popperfoto) pp. 30, 46, 59, *(London Times)* p. 39, *(Express Newspapers/ F11BJ5D)* p. 56, (Max Miller/Fotos International) p. 81, (Reuters/ Enrique Shore) p. 115; UPI/Corbis-Bettmann, pp. 28, 33, 52, 70, 92; © FPG International LLC, p. 35; © AP/Wide World Photos, pp. 60, 83, 90, 104, 114; © *Sports Illustrated,* p. 65; © Russ Adams Productions, Inc., pp. 68, 76, 84, 89; Women's Sports Foundation, p. 97; © Carol L. Newsom, pp. 102, 106, 108, 112, 118 (both); R. D. O'Neal, p. 128.

Cover photographs by Carol L. Newsom.

A B O U T   T H E   A U T H O R

Joanne Lannin is a feature writer for a daily newspaper in Maine. She has written extensively about athletes and other celebrities. Ms. Lannin received a bachelor's degree in English from the University of New Hampshire and a master's degree in journalism from Boston University. An avid athlete, she plays tennis, softball, and basketball and coaches middle school basketball.

Other Lerner Biographies of interest:
Muhammad Ali: Champion
Ray Charles: Soul Man
The 14th Dalai Lama: Spiritual Leader of Tibet
Sir Edmund Hillary: To Everest and Beyond
Marilyn Monroe: Norma Jeane's Dream
Steven Spielberg: Master Storyteller
Gloria Steinem: Feminist at Large
Aung San Suu Kyi: Fearless Voice of Burma